How to establish
financial

Biblical Solutions to Manage Your Money •

security

OLUMIDE EMMANUEL

DESTINY IMAGE™ EUROPE srl
Via Maiella, 1
66020 San Giovanni Teatino (Ch) - Italy

"Changing the world, one book at a time."

This book and all other Destiny Image™ Europe books are available at Christian bookstores and distributors worldwide.

To order products, or for any other correspondence:

DESTINY IMAGE™ EUROPE srl
Via Acquacorrente, 6
65123 - Pescara - Italy
Tel. +39 085 4716623 - Fax +39 085 9431270
E-mail: info@eurodestinyimage.com

Or reach us on the Internet: **www.eurodestinyimage.com**

ISBN: 978-88-89127-79-7
For Worldwide Distribution, Printed in the U.S.A.
1 2 3 4 5 6 7 8/13 12 11 10 09

Dedication

This book is specially dedicated to all the past and present members of Calvary Bible Church. For over a decade, I have taught these principles in your midst and seen results. You were my field of experimentation. And to all those in different nations of the world who have sat under my teaching on wealth creation and produced results, thanks for proving that it works. *I love you all!*

Acknowledgments

Emulation is the starting point of education, and we are all products of what we have learned through various channels in life. I want to start by saluting all the great teachers and authors whom I have had the privilege to sit under or read from. You are numerous, and space will not permit me to mention you each by name. But you have all blessed me and are part of this book.

To my parents, mentors, friends, members, partners, staff, and supporters, I say thank you. Thanks also to the whole team at Destiny Image Europe, and to my wife and our unique children. Finally, thanks to the God of all flesh, the Master of the universe, the Lover of my soul, my eternal inspiration, to whom all honor and glory is due. Daddy in Heaven, Almighty God, my comfort, I give thanks for the inspiration, grace, wisdom, provision, sustenance, and breakthrough You have given this book. It's all about You, Lord! I love you!

Endorsements

Previous books and other teaching materials by Pastor Olumide Emmanuel have made a tremendous impact on me and my ministry. He has a unique grace to challenge people to fulfill their destiny and defeat poverty. This book will surely bless every reader.

Pastor Mike Adebiyi
Jubilee Christian Center
Atlanta, Georgia

Olumide Emmanuel is a prolific author, speaker, and entrepreneur who has written and spoken on various topics that concern living victoriously daily. This book is another one from his arsenal that teaches on how you can create the wealth that is very much needed to fund kingdom projects and advancement.

Dr. Sola Fola Alade
Pastor of Trinity Chapel (RCCG), London
Publisher of Leadership & Lifestyle Magazine

I have known Pastor Olumide for nearly two decades as a man of integrity and purpose. This is a must-read book because it is a practical representation of those principles that God has used through Pastor Olumide to positively influence the lives of many. It is your turn.

Pastor Lekan W. Adegunwa
The Reconciliation Ministries and House of Mercy
United Kingdom

Pastor Olumide is an awesome revelator and tremendous international speaker. His insight on wealth building and economic mobility by using kingdom principles has been revolutionary. To chronicle this wisdom will be a standing reference for all those that are trusting God for increase, but increase will not come without strategic information. Pastor Olumide has been anointed to inform and educate. I believe this book, filled with the great revelation God has given him, will change the way we think, act, and access wealth in the Kingdom. "God has given us the power to get wealth." (See Deuteronomy 8:18.)

Bishop Mitchell G. Taylor
Senior Pastor of Center of Hope International
Long Island, New York

Pastor Olumide Emmanuel is one of the few voices that give practical, scriptural instructions on the effective Kingdom way of becoming wealthy. His approach on issues is always balanced, especially in this age of extremes. I strongly believe that this book will be a tremendous blessing to you. For those who are struggling with poverty, the biblical principles in this book will make you rich—and make those who are rich wealthy.

Pastor Sam Ore
Author and Senior Pastor
Kingdom Ambassador Christian Center
Greenbelt, Maryland

How to Establish Financial Security is a thorough guide to acquiring and maintaining wealth. It is a well-written book, simple yet dynamic in its content. The author has shared his experiences and strategies not only as a teacher and a minister but also as a shrewd businessman keen to share his knowledge on the subject of acquiring and maintaining wealth. This book has passed on an abundance of golden nuggets of wisdom that I have found eminently useful. In my opinion, it is the perfect investment to make in this era of financial crises.

Kenny Adeshugba
Senior Pastor of Charis Christian Centre
London, United Kingdom

Pastor Emmanuel's approach to wealth creation is both practical and effective. I highly recommend this resource to all who are serious about discovering a financial strategy that works.

Dr. Derek Grier
Bishop of Grace Church
Dumfries, Virginia

Olumide Emmanuel is again in the charts with a best seller. This masterpiece, like his other books, combines deep knowledge and understanding on the subject matter. I personally recommend this timely piece to all Christians, non-Christians, and people in the corporate world. Bravo, Olumide, for this amazing work in a time like this!

Pastor Yaw Boadi
Association of African Caribbean Ministers in France

Thinking about it, Olumide Emmanuel is unquestionably qualified to bring this powerful, profound, and yet simple truth to us all. He has lived, proved, and taught many the fact that your present situation shouldn't be your destination and that there is a pathway to wealth for all who are willing to pursue and live by the principles shared in this volume. He is a man of integrity and proven success over the years. Let's thank him that he has chosen to share these powerful truths with us all.

Dr. David Sola Oludoye
Royal Connections, United Kingdom

Pastor Olumide Emmanuel is a timely gift to the Kingdom of God and wider society, which is why his ministry has diligently and progressively impacted countless lives with profound wisdom and truth. *How to Establish Financial Security* is a phenomenal book unleashed with practical principles and guidelines on how to advance in business and finance.

Pastor Phillip Thomas
Senior Pastor of Better Life Assembly
Kent, England

Behind every success story there is a secret. True success proceeds from God; even then, there is a pathway to God. In the dawn of a collapsing global economy, where former billionaires are contemplating suicide gripped by the fear of what is to come, there is the need to truly ask oneself, how true and stable is the path that I am pursuing? There has never been a better stage for the righteous to arise and shine as the stars of Heaven than the current climate.

But how? In a balanced presentation of prudence and righteousness, Olumide Emmanuel has demonstrated that not only does God want you to have good success, but he has also shown the pathway to that end. This is a must-read for all without greed!

Pastor Wale Olulana
Senior Pastor of Harmony Christian Centre
London, United Kingdom

Table of Contents

Foreword

I am so overwhelmed with joy to have such a good friend as Olumide Emmanuel and also to go through his book, *How to Establish Financial Security*. I think that Olumide is a humble servant of God and a jewel that is hidden in the soil of Nigeria, yet to be discovered. Despite the many gifted ministers we have in Nigeria, I have come to see that this modest man is specifically and uniquely gifted with the word of wisdom for this nation.

Pastor Olumide Emmanuel is not religious at all! He is so radical in his thinking, and it's only this mind-set that will set Nigeria free. It is only this kind of teaching, which is practical and not superficial, that can really help people to come away from the hook of satan and poverty and into their promised land.

His books, *Common Sense Is Not Common* and *Are You a Fool?* show us that wisdom is the principle thing of life. However, the best and most relevant topic for our people and all the suffering people of the world is *How to Establish Financial Security*.

My friends, I beckon you, *please take this book seriously!* I agree with the author that the path to prosperity is not through giving only. It is necessary for the teaching of doctrine first, to till the ground. Then we must cultivate and develop the soil, namely the territory that is given to us, which has the potential to produce all that we could hope and dream of in the form of a harvest.

There is no wealth and prosperity without producing goods and services. We have to give goods and offer services in exchange for money and wealth. Without producing goods and services, it is naive and absurd to ever think that we could achieve financial freedom.

Through this book, there is no doubt that if you practice the principles laid out here, you will surely come to abundance and prosperity—even in Africa, and regardless of the land or country where you reside.

Prosperity is a reality, as Olumide Emmanuel has spoken to us so clearly through this wonderful book. I very much appreciate this brilliant work from an anointed and inspiring man of God. I would like to wish him "more grease to his elbow!"

May God strengthen him and use him to bring freedom and liberty to the people of Nigeria and to the countries of the world!

Yours in Him.

Pastor Sunday Adelaja
The Embassy of the Blessed Kingdom
of God for All Nations
Kiev, Ukraine

Introduction

The labor of fools wearies them, for they do not even know how to go to the city! (Ecclesiastes 10:15)

If laboring were the way to become wealthy, there would only be a few poor people on earth. Many people labor endlessly and yet remain poor because they do not know *how* to translate their labor into wealth. Hard work must be accompanied by smart work for labor to produce the expected profit. Many want to become rich and wealthy, but they do not know how.

Many people know *what* they want but do not know *how* to get it. If there is one thing that has caused the greatest problems for people in life, it is the issue of money.

- Those who do not have it hunger and crave it.
- Those who have it press for more of it.
- Those who do not know how to handle it end up mourning.

While the lack or absence of money has brought great sorrow to many, the hunger and craze for it has also been the undoing of some. The love of money is a deadly disease, and poverty is also a deadly disease. Money matters are at the root of many vices in the world today—from robbery to assassination, corruption to prostitution, separation and divorce between couples and business partners, and so on. Even in religious circles, money often plays a major role in betrayals, rejections, and disloyalties that occur. Compromise has become second nature in the Church because of money.

As bad as these issues have become, one major enemy that has been ignored—regardless of its power and its ability to cause damage—is "the religious spirit." This spirit has caused great damage in the Church and in the world at large. It is a very dangerous spirit, even more dangerous than the devil, because it causes its captives to self-destruct. It has kept many from what rightfully belongs to them. Instead of being distributors of wealth, we are busy contending for "the wealth of the wicked."

Today in the Church, we talk about wealth transfer and wealth of the wicked, and one begins to wonder: Was wealth created for the wicked? Who gave wealth to them? Was it like that in the beginning? Who was in control of wealth in the Garden of Eden? Was it the righteous or the wicked? Even if we were to partake of wealth transfer, *how* would this be achieved?

This is a how-to book; the mission of this book is to:

- Set in motion the total eradication of poverty.

- Reveal wisdom, common sense principles, and strategies for wealth creation.

- Reveal economic principles for making, managing, and multiplying money.

- Activate every reader's ability to make money, by developing in each reader an investment mentality.

- Reveal the pathway that leads to wealth so every reader can make the trip.

- Help replace generational curses with generational blessings.

- Raise investors and entrepreneurs for the 21st century.

Get ready for the journey of a lifetime. Fasten your seat belt and get ready to make the trip to the place of wealth as you discover *How to Establish Financial Security*. I have included a workbook for you to use either as you finish each chapter or as a review after you reach the end of the book.

Before going any further, please take a few moments to complete the Financial Intelligence Questionnaire (FIQ). This will provide a good starting point for our discussion of financial security.

Congratulations in advance as you begin the journey to a place of wealth. Shalom.

Financial Intelligence Questionnaire (FIQ)

Please answer *yes, no,* or *I don't know* to each of the following questions. Be sure to keep track of your answers.

1. Do you know your present financial condition or net worth?

   ☐ yes   ☐ no   ☐ I don't know

2. Are you satisfied with your present financial condition?

   ☐ yes   ☐ no   ☐ I don't know

3. Are you aware of the simple ways to increase your net worth?

   ☐ yes   ☐ no   ☐ I don't know

4. Do you have enough savings to see you through six months of normal living expenses if you lose your job?

   ☐ yes   ☐ no   ☐ I don't know

5. Do you save money on a regular basis?

☐ yes   ☐ no   ☐ I don't know

6. Have you developed the habit of saving?

☐ yes   ☐ no   ☐ I don't know

7. Do you have a well-defined, documented financial goal?

☐ yes   ☐ no   ☐ I don't know

8. Do you have a bank account?

☐ yes   ☐ no   ☐ I don't know

9. Do you reconcile your bank statements every month?

☐ yes   ☐ no   ☐ I don't know

10. Do you keep a record of your income and expenditures?

☐ yes   ☐ no   ☐ I don't know

11. Do you know how much you spend each month?

☐ yes   ☐ no   ☐ I don't know

12. Do you spend less than you earn?

☐ yes   ☐ no   ☐ I don't know

13. Do you have a household budget, and are you successful at managing it?

☐ yes   ☐ no   ☐ I don't know

14. Do you avoid major credit purchases?

☐ yes ☐ no ☐ I don't know

15. Do you take advantage of all savings and investment opportunities that come your way?

☐ yes ☐ no ☐ I don't know

16. Do you have any investment that helps to reduce your taxable income?

☐ yes ☐ no ☐ I don't know

17. Do you diversify your investments?

☐ yes ☐ no ☐ I don't know

18. Are you satisfied with the contribution from your investment to your total income?

☐ yes ☐ no ☐ I don't know

19. Do you feel you have a brilliant financial adviser or team of advisers?

☐ yes ☐ no ☐ I don't know

20. Do you feel you have sufficient life insurance coverage?

☐ yes ☐ no ☐ I don't know

21. Do you have a plan for your children's college or university education?

☐ yes ☐ no ☐ I don't know

22. Do you own a house?

☐ yes ☐ no ☐ I don't know

23. Do you have a plan to retire in comfort?

☐ yes ☐ no ☐ I don't know

24. Have you prepared your will?

☐ yes ☐ no ☐ I don't know

25. Are you in control of your financial future?

☐ yes ☐ no ☐ I don't know

26. Are you satisfied with the contribution you have made to the world?

☐ yes ☐ no ☐ I don't know

SCORING

Add up how many questions you answered *no* or *I don't know*. If your total is:

0 to 4	You are in good shape—keep it up.
5 to 10	You are on the right track, but there is room for improvement.
11 to 12	You have a weak pulse—you need revival.
13 or higher	You need a life.

Chapter I

Poverty Redefined

*Many people look but only
a few people see.*

MY STORY

I was a child of God, yet I was financially poor. I was a Christian, yet I was financially poor. I was anointed, yet I was financially poor. I was a pastor, yet I was financially poor. I was living right, yet I was financially poor. I was a doer of the Word, yet I was financially poor. I was a tither, yet I was financially poor. I was a giver, yet I was financially poor.

I am still all of the above, but financially my story has changed. This book is a result of an encounter that changed my story. It all began in the mid-1990s, but it came to a climax in 1998 when I reached a point of frustration.

I was born again as a teenager and ordained as a pastor at the age of twentyone. By twentyfour, I was already a senior pastor of the church where I am still privileged to pastor today. All my life I have been a practitioner of the Word, and I endeavor to practice all I have been taught or learned.

With all this, I expected that my finances would improve "even as my soul prospered," but the reverse seemed to be the case. Being a full-time pastor with full-time responsibilities but no full-time rewards made my life miserable financially, and I became frustrated.

The birth of my first child—a beautiful, precious miracle from God—coupled with some other things that happened during this period of my life, got me thinking. In my frustration I cried out to God for divine intervention to change my story. I quoted all kinds of Scriptures to God and asked Him why all these Bible verses were not a reality in my life, regardless of my years of service and commitment to Him and His Word. God's answer shocked me. In response to all the Scriptures I quoted, I kept hearing in my spirit, "Who told you?"

For the first time in my life I realized that even though I was doing the right things, I was not doing them by revelation but by religion. I was sowing because I was taught to, and I wanted a harvest, not because I had perfect understanding. I was paying tithes because I was taught to, and I was afraid of the devourer.

That encounter with God took me on an eight-month journey in obedience to God. I was inspired to study the Bible all over again, to get a personal revelation from God for everything I was to continue to do. I read many books on finances, written by major ministers of the Gospel, to discover what they taught about the pathway to wealth. I studied religion to determine how Christianity is being practiced today.

My journey of obedience transformed my life and ministry completely and changed my financial story. Three years after this encounter, I left the poverty zone forever. I am now on a divine mission to teach others what I discovered, to help them exit the poverty zone. This book is a tool to achieve that aim.

I no longer *pay* tithes; I now *give* tithes because I love the Lord—not because I am afraid of the devourer. I give more than I have before, and now I give because I love God. I am Kingdom-minded and know harvest will come. I am still a Christian, but I am completely free from religion. Now I realize that Christianity is not religion but a way of life.

I have come to recognize that imbalance is a major problem in the Church, and extremes are the norm. Over 90 percent of the books I read on finances by Christian authors reveal that the only way to prosper is by giving and sowing, which is what many have been doing without result. Only a few authors teach balanced biblical wealth creation strategy. Giving alone is not the way to prosper and create wealth. Kingdom wealth is not created; it is entrusted to us by God. Though spiritual investment to wealth is a major focus of many churches, physical investment to wealth is often ignored.

Both spiritual and physical investment come together to form the pathway to wealth creation, and one is not complete without the other. Spiritual investment is the *foundation* and *security* of physical investment, while physical investment is the *completion* and *glory* of all spiritual investment.

You may presently be frustrated by your financial status, but rejoice because your story is about to change. You may have been paying tithes, yet things are tight. You may have been giving offerings, yet you are suffering. You may have been laboring yet have no visible result.

Weep no more, because the God who did it for me will do it for you. This book is your passport to financial freedom. May you become a testimony like the many whom this information has transformed.

WHAT IS POVERTY?

Nothing is as sadly amusing as hearing a poor person declare, "I am not poor." Many people tend to define poverty and prosperity in terms of money alone, losing sight of deeper truths. Are you poor? This chapter should help you gain a better and clearer understanding of poverty.

Poverty Is a State of Lack or Hardship

When a person is in a state of lack or hardship, he or she is said to be in poverty. To the extent that one lacks what is vital, one is poor. This refers to more than just money. We know that when someone is lacking money, they may be viewed as being in poverty. But the same holds true when we are lacking other vital elements, such as lack of positive relationships, lack of good health, or lack of faith in God. Whatever good thing we lack should be sought after in order to change our status. If you presently lack money and things are hard for you, relax—your present state is not your final status.

Poverty Is a Mentality

A poverty mentality is one of the most dangerous aspects of poverty. It is the reason why many are not wealthy. It is the reason why many consume all they have without setting aside for savings or investment.

Imagine if you were given the option to choose between getting 1 million dollars now or getting one dollar compounded at a rate of 100 percent per month over thirty months. Which would you choose? A poverty mentality would choose getting 1 million immediately, but an investment mentality would choose the latter. One dollar compounded at 100 percent per month over thirty months will amount to well over 500 million dollars!

Poverty Is a Curse

The next two descriptions may sound spiritual or religious, but they are part of the definition of poverty. Many are poor today and will remain poor because they are operating under the curse of poverty. A *curse* by definition is something that "causes harm, misfortune, or failure." Failure at the brink of a miracle, "almost there" syndrome, near-success failures, constant disappointment, limitations, lack of achievement, deprivation, and hardship are all characteristics of one who is under the curse of poverty.

Poverty Is a Spirit

The physical realm is controlled by the spiritual. Many times when you see someone living in abject poverty, it is because the spirit of poverty has attached itself to them. The spirit of poverty is no respecter of age, status, color, qualifications, title, or location. I am presently writing this chapter from a hotel room in New York, and looking through the window I can see a man dressed in rags pushing a cart of trash down the street. There are poor people everywhere. The spirit of poverty attaches itself to people like a garment, and until removed it continues to keep one in poverty.

The descriptions of poverty we have examined reveal that there are different aspects to poverty. These descriptions help to categorize poverty into different types and dimensions beyond the general monetary definition.

Dimensions of Poverty

There are many dimensions of poverty. Let's take the time to define some of them:

- *Financial poverty* is the general dimension of poverty known to many; it refers to a lack of money or material assets.

- *Mental poverty* is a poverty of ideas. When you have money but are lacking ideas, you can end up losing your money. To be barren of ideas is a terrible poverty.

- *Social poverty* refers to having money but not having anyone with whom to enjoy it. A life that is barren of good relationships is a frustrating life. Social poverty is also referred to as *relational poverty*.

- *Physical poverty* includes living in bad health and being physically poor. Just as the saying "health is wealth" is true, lack of good health to enjoy life is real poverty.

- *Achievement poverty* involves living a life void of any meaningful progress, success, or achievement. Imagine the following obituary: "He was born, he lived, and he died." A life summarized in such a way—without impact on one's generation—is a futile and poor life. Such a person did not live; he simply existed.

- *Knowledge poverty* includes lacking knowledge, information, or skills to achieve progress.

- *Spiritual poverty* means lacking faith and a covenant relationship with God. This is real poverty because—after all is said and done—there is life after death, and money or material possessions are useless in that realm. Only faith in God through His Son Jesus matters.

Are you poor? Hopefully, you realize now that poverty refers to more than simply monetary status. Many people are poor and remain poor because they do not know why they are poor. When people do not know what causes their poverty, they continue in ignorance and remain in poverty. If we keep doing things the way we have been doing them, we will continue to get the same results. Let us move on to examine the universal causes of poverty in order to find the way out.

Chapter 2

Universal Causes of Poverty

*Poverty is not a respecter of person, age,
color, title, race, place, or religion.*

Let's travel briefly into the world of imagination. Imagine a man trying to operate an electronic gadget without making any progress. He tries all the buttons and does all he can do but still cannot successfully operate the gadget. After much effort, he picks up the manual only to discover that he has ignored the first and most important step: plug the gadget into an electric outlet. How can an electronic gadget function when it is not connected to electricity? When the gadget is connected, the man's efforts produce results. His earlier efforts were not wrong, but they could not produce results due to an underlying problem: disconnection from the power source.

Many people are like this man. They do everything they can but still remain poor because they are disconnected from what could change their story. They ignore the information manual that could turn their situation around. To become rich or wealthy, first we have to discover why we are poor.

The question to ask is not, "What can I do to be rich and wealthy?" but rather, "Why am I not rich and wealthy?" Many spend their lives wondering and searching for what they can do to be rich and wealthy instead of finding out why they are not rich and wealthy and dealing with the obstacles to riches and wealth.

In my few years of researching why people all over the world are poor, I have discovered some universal reasons for poverty and lack. Regardless of location, poverty comes as a result of different reasons, which fall under seven categories. We will look at each in turn.

IGNORANCE

My people are destroyed for lack of knowledge. Because you have rejected knowledge, I also will reject you from being priest for Me; because you have forgotten the law of your God, I also will forget your children (Hosea 4:6).

I am sure you have heard the expression "Knowledge is power." Well, just as knowledge is power, ignorance is deadly. Many people are in the school of ignorance, and this is the root of poverty in their lives. As I go from nation to nation, observing people who are poor, I see that they all fall under one or more kinds of ignorance.

Ignorance of Who They Are

Many people are poor because they are ignorant of who they are. In the movie *The Prince and the Pauper*, a prince and a pauper exchange places and pretend to be that which they are not. Even though they exchange roles, it is difficult for them to adjust to their new circumstances. The prince finds it hard to adjust to the lifestyle of a pauper because in his heart and mind he knows he is a prince. In the same way, the pauper has trouble fully enjoying living like a prince.

Their mind-sets influence their role-playing. At times, their attitudes and actions reveal who they really are. The prince knows who he is, and hence he cannot fully surrender to a life of shame and reproach. In the same way, we must know who we are in God. As we discover the real us as intended by the Creator, it will then be difficult to settle for a life of poverty and hardship.

Ignorance of What They Have

Undiscovered potential is useless potential. Many are poor and stay poor because they are ignorant of what they have. We can see this in several examples from the Bible: Moses and his rod, the widow and her pot of oil, Adam and his divine connection (see Exod. 3–4; 1 Kings 17; Gen. 1–3).

It reminds me of the story of a man who desired to travel from his home country and seek greener pastures in a foreign land. He sold all he had to buy passage on a ship. As the ship left port, he locked himself in his cabin with two bottles of water and a pack of biscuits, and he stayed there for the entire duration of the journey. After a few weeks, a steward knocked on the man's door to invite him to the final banquet before arrival, but he was too weak to open the door. When the steward forced the door open, he saw a man close to death from hunger and dehydration. When asked why he never came out to eat during the journey, the man replied that he had no money to pay for food. The shocked steward explained that the ticket the man had purchased entitled him to three free meals daily for the duration of the journey. The man was too weak, too shocked, and too disappointed to react. No matter what he ate now, this was the final banquet; it could not make up for all he had lost through his ignorance.

Many go through life like this ignorant man. They are born crying; they live suffering; they die disappointed. This happens because they are ignorant of what rightfully belongs to them. *What do you have? What rightfully belongs to you?*

Ignorance of What They Can Do

Some people say things like, "I have done all I know how to do without result. What else do you want me to do?" or "I don't know what to do anymore." Many stay poor because they do not know what they can do or what they are supposed to do. That is why this book exists. It is meant to help people know what they can do to change their financial situation and move from poverty to prosperity. *What can you do?*

Ignorance of What They Should Avoid

There are many poverty-promoting mind-sets, habits, attitudes, and lifestyles that may hinder any person. It is important to know where the danger lies so we can avoid it. If we are struggling, we must learn what things to avoid in order to break free from poverty. This book should help shed light on these issues.

Ignorance of Wealth Creation Principles and Strategies

If everyone knew which steps to take to become rich and wealthy, many would take them. Ignorance of universal wealth creation principles and strategies has been the undoing of many. Amazingly, due to a poverty mentality, many do not invest in materials that could help them understand these principles and strategies. We have had the privilege to organize numerous wealth creation seminars, but often those who seem to need them most are absent. Even when the seminars are free, many are too busy to attend. There are countless books, tapes, seminars, and CDs that reveal various wealth creation principles and strategies, but you must be willing to invest some time and money to learn from them.

The Example of King Solomon

When Solomon became king, he had a conversation with God:

> *On that night God appeared to Solomon, and said to him, "Ask! What shall I give you?" And Solomon said to God: "You have shown great mercy to David my father, and have made me king in his place.... Now give me wisdom and knowledge, that I may go out and come in before this people..."* (2 Chronicles 1:7-8;10).

How did God respond to Solomon?

> *Then God said to Solomon: "Because this was in your heart, and you have not asked riches or wealth or honor...but have asked wisdom and knowledge for yourself, that you may judge My people over whom I have made you king—wisdom and knowledge are granted to you; and I will give you riches and wealth and honor, such as none of the kings have had who were before you, nor shall any after you have the like"* (2 Chronicles 1:11-12).

To avoid or escape ignorance, we must seek wisdom and knowledge. This includes knowing who we are in Christ, what we have (our potential), what we can do, what we should avoid, and what tools are available to help us. Now that we have examined ignorance—the first universal cause of poverty—let's move on.

LAZINESS

The Book of Ecclesiastes warns that "Because of laziness the building decays, and through idleness of hands the house leaks" (Eccles. 10:18). And throughout the Book of Proverbs, we read how laziness is a cause of poverty. But what is laziness? Let's look at some of its attributes.

The Danger of Idleness and Procrastination

Lazy people are often idle and procrastinate. They put off until later what they could do today; they refuse to act promptly. Let's look at what Proverbs says about this. "He who has a slack hand becomes poor, but the hand of the diligent makes rich. He who gathers in summer is a wise son; he who sleeps in harvest is a son who causes shame" (Prov. 10:4-5). Another version says, "Lazy hands make a man poor" (see Prov. 10:4 NIV).

Later in Proverbs we read, "The hand of the diligent will rule, but the lazy man will be put to forced labor.... The lazy man does not roast what he took in hunting, but diligence is man's precious possession" (Prov. 12:24;27). This is an amazing revelation. How can a man who has gone hunting still be called lazy? He is lazy because he hunted, but he did not roast or process what he caught. Raw material is like undiscovered potential—both are useless until they are discovered and turned into something useful. It is not good to eat raw meat, so hunting is useless if the meat is allowed to spoil due to lack of roasting or preservation.

Can you see now that procrastination is part of laziness? What could you do that you have not yet done? Many nations and individuals are like this lazy man; they stop at the raw-material phase. No wonder nations like Nigeria still struggle. Nigeria, for example, sells crude oil to others to process. Then Nigeria buys back the refined (processed) oil at many times the original crude selling price. Imagine if Nigeria processed oil for its own use.

The Danger of Too Much Sleep

Let's look again at Proverbs to see what it says about laziness and sleep.

Laziness casts one into a deep sleep, and an idle person will suffer hunger.... The lazy man will not plow because of winter; he will beg during harvest and have nothing.... Do not love sleep, lest you come to poverty; open your eyes, and you will be satisfied with bread (Proverbs 19:15; 20:4,13).

The lessons here are self-evident:

- Too much sleep is a trademark of a lazy person.
- Laziness leads to idleness and ends in hunger.
- Lazy people often give excuses.
- Lazy people may resort to begging.

Proverbs chapter 24 clearly describes how small but continual acts of laziness can lead to poverty catching you off guard and unaware:

I went by the field of the lazy man, and by the vineyard of the man devoid of understanding; and there it was, all overgrown with thorns; its surface was covered with nettles; its stone wall was broken down. When I saw it, I considered it well; I looked on it and received instruction: A little sleep, a little slumber, a little folding of the hands to rest; so shall your poverty come like a prowler, and your need like an armed man (Proverbs 24:30-34).

The Danger of Excuses

Lazy people are full of excuses; that is a primary trademark. They often have excuses for their situation or condition. They often blame others for their state. They often have a victim or entitlement mentality.

Do you see a man wise in his own eyes? There is more hope for a fool than for him. The lazy man says, "There is a lion in the road! A fierce lion is in the streets!" As a door turns on its hinges, so does the lazy man on his bed. The lazy man buries his hand in the bowl; it wearies him to bring it back to his mouth. The lazy man is wiser in his own eyes than seven men who can answer sensibly (Proverbs 26:12-16).

Lazy people can be amusing. How did that lazy man know there was lion in the street when he had not left his home? He was making an excuse so he could stay home and stay in bed.

To avoid poverty, we must guard against becoming lazy. This means we should avoid idleness and procrastination, we should take care not to sleep or rest too much, and we should watch that we do not make excuses that lead to inaction. Now it is time to look at another cause of poverty: unfaithfulness.

UNFAITHFULNESS

Have you noticed how difficult it has become to find faithful people today? Even in church, the story is the same. Many seem to have a covenant with poverty—every time an opportunity to change their story appears, they end up messing it up. Are you faithful? Can you be trusted? Are you dependable? I cannot begin to tell you stories of people I know whose situation would have been better if only they had been faithful with the opportunity they had.

I know of many people today who have money to invest but only need faithful people to trust. Let's once again learn from Proverbs. In Proverbs chapter 11, we read that unfaithfulness leads to destruction and that the lust of the unfaithful will cause them to fall or fail.

> *The integrity of the upright will guide them, but the perversity of the unfaithful will destroy them.... The righteousness of the upright will deliver them, but the unfaithful will be caught by their lust* (Proverbs 11:3,6).

In Proverbs chapter 13, we see that those who are unfaithful may be prone to violence. We also see that unfaithfulness leads to hardship.

> *A man shall eat well by the fruit of his mouth, but the soul of the unfaithful feeds on violence.... Good understanding gains favor, but the way of the unfaithful is hard* (Proverbs 13:2,15).

Finally, in Proverbs chapter 25 we read that unfaithful people are undependable and unreliable. "Confidence in an unfaithful man in time of trouble is like a bad tooth and a foot out of joint" (Prov. 25:19).

After reading these descriptions of unfaithfulness, do you think an unfaithful man can ever become rich and wealthy? I doubt it. Even if he does become rich, it will not last. I have never seen an armed robber who retired successfully and handed over his "earnings" to the next generation. As it says in Proverbs, "Wealth gained by dishonesty will be diminished, but he who gathers by labor will increase" (Prov. 13:11).

Dishonesty and unfaithfulness is not the way to become rich and wealthy. Whenever you have an opportunity to be in a place of responsibility, all that is required of you is to be faithful. As it says in the Book of Luke:

> *He who is faithful in what is least is faithful also in much; and he who is unjust in what is least is unjust also in much. Therefore if you have not been faithful in the unrighteous mammon, who will commit to your trust the true riches? And if you have not been faithful in what is another man's, who will give you what is your own? No servant can serve two masters; for either he will hate the one and love the other, or else he will be loyal to the one and despise the other. You cannot serve God and mammon (Luke 16:10-13).*

If we are unfaithful in little, we will be unfaithful in much. If we are unfaithful in matters as mundane as money and material possessions, we will not be entrusted with divine and spiritual valuables. If we are unfaithful in the way we handle other people's belongings, we will not have our own. Many are poor today because of their unfaithfulness.

PRIDE

I have seen many people stay jobless due to pride. Pride is the reason for poverty in many lives. Proud people are unteachable and refuse to follow instructions that could deliver them from destruction. Proud people always avoid starting small or starting from where they are because they have delusions of grandeur. For example, if you want a corporate job, then you should have a corporate certificate and the necessary qualifications. You should not just assume that you can start at the top.

Let's look to the Bible and see what we can learn about pride. First, we see that God does not like pride, and He keeps His distance from those who are prideful.

> *Whoever secretly slanders his neighbor, him I will destroy; the one who has a haughty look and a proud heart, him I will not endure....Though the Lord is on high, yet He regards the lowly; but the proud He knows from afar (Psalms 101:5; 138:6).*

Next, we read of the negative fallout from pride. Pride results in shame and strife. "When pride comes, then comes shame; but with the humble is wisdom.... By pride comes nothing but strife, but with the well-advised is wisdom" (Prov. 11:2; 13:10).

Pride produces nothing good. Even when proud people succeed in gathering wealth and riches, the riches do not last because God brings such people down to the place of humiliation. As it says in Proverbs, "The Lord will destroy the house of the proud.... Everyone proud in heart is an abomination to the Lord; though they join forces, none will go unpunished" (Prov. 15:25; 16:5). Pride will bring a man low, and that is why it is a major cause of poverty.

> *"The pride of your heart has deceived you, you who dwell in the clefts of the rock, whose habitation is high; you who say in your heart, 'Who will bring me down to the ground?' Though you ascend as high as the eagle, and though you set your nest among the stars, from there I will bring you down," says the Lord* (Obadiah 1:3-4).

Whoa! What a great danger pride poses to us. Pride is deceptive and, as we have just read, there is no escape from poverty for a proud man. We read in First John that pride is not of God but of the world, and God will have nothing to do with a proud person.

> *Do not love the world or the things in the world. If anyone loves the world, the love of the Father is not in him. For all that is in the world—the lust of the flesh, the lust of the eyes, and the pride of life—is not of the Father but is of the world. And the world is passing away, and the lust of it; but he who does the will of God abides forever* (1 John 2:15-17).

God stands against and resists any proud person. As it says in James, 'God resists the proud, but gives grace to the humble' (see James 4:6). When we are proud, God stands as an obstacle to our progress, and if God is against us, who can help us?

If we find ourselves in that position, what should we do? The answer lies in Scripture. The Book of James says, "Humble yourselves in the sight of the Lord, and He will lift you up" (James 4:10). And in Proverbs we read, "A man's pride will bring him low, but the humble in spirit will retain honor" (Prov. 29:23). Wisdom demands that we steer clear of pride and humble ourselves so that God can lift us up and promote us to the place of abundance.

DISOBEDIENCE

Who would let employees disobey all instructions and rules, live and operate any way they like, and then still continually promote them? I doubt if any of us would. If disobedient employees are not promoted, why do we expect to disobey God and still receive His blessings? Disobedience has kept many people away from a place of wealth. There are two dimensions of disobedience I have observed that keep people poor throughout the world:

- Disobedience to God's commandments and instructions.

- Disobedience to wealth creation principles and laws.

In Isaiah we read, "'If you are willing and obedient, you shall eat the good of the land; but if you refuse and rebel, you shall be devoured by the sword'; for the mouth of the Lord has spoken" (Isa. 1:19-20). These verses state that there are two conditions that must be met in order to partake of the good of the land; we must be *willing* and *obedient*. I have observed that many are willing, but only a few are obedient. Willingness is not enough. We must obey the laws and principles that produce the good of the land.

In Job it says, "If they obey and serve Him, they shall spend their days in prosperity, and their years in pleasures. But if they do not obey, they shall perish by the sword, and they shall die without knowledge" (Job 36:11-12). Here again, we see two conditions for prosperity; we must *serve* and *obey*. Some people claim to serve God, but only on their own terms. They disobey any of God's instructions that do not feel good to their flesh. Serving without obedience is a capital offense. Serving and obeying, however, makes us candidates for divine prosperity and a lifetime of pleasure.

> *"Now it shall come to pass, if you diligently obey the voice of the Lord your God, to observe carefully all His commandments which I command you today, that the Lord your God will set you high above all nations of the earth. And all these blessings shall come*

*upon you and overtake you, because you obey the voice of the Lord
your God"* (Deuteronomy 28:1-2).

Obedience is the key to God's blessings. Read Deuteronomy 28:3-14
to see a list of all the blessings attached to obedience. We cannot be obedient and still remain poor.

Looking further in Deuteronomy chapter 28, beginning with verse
15, we see a warning about disobedience:

> *"But it shall come to pass, if you do not obey the voice of the Lord
> your God, to observe carefully all His commandments and His
> statutes which I command you today, that all these curses will
> come upon you and overtake you"* (Deuteronomy 28:15).

Verses 16 through 68 of Deuteronomy chapter 28 contain a terrible
description of what disobedience can bring to a man's life. We cannot
live in disobedience and still become all that God wants us to be.

First Samuel 15 says that obedience delights the Lord more than
sacrifice and describes the consequences of Saul's disobedience:

> *So Samuel said: "Has the Lord as great delight in burnt offerings
> and sacrifices, as in obeying the voice of the Lord? Behold, to obey
> is better than sacrifice, and to heed than the fat of rams. For rebel-
> lion is as the sin of witchcraft, and stubbornness is as iniquity and
> idolatry. Because you have rejected the word of the Lord, He also
> has rejected you from being king"* (1 Samuel 15:22-23).

I encourage you to read the entire fifteenth chapter of First Samuel
to gain a complete picture of Saul's journey of disobedience. It is better
to obey God than to bribe Him with the proceeds of your disobedience. Many think they are obedient because they do not realize that:

- Delayed obedience is disobedience.

- Partial obedience is disobedience.

- Adjusted obedience is disobedience.

- Incomplete obedience is disobedience.

Jeremiah chapter 11 describes the outcomes of disobedience and
obedience:

The word that came to Jeremiah from the Lord, saying, "Hear the words of this covenant, and speak to the men of Judah and to the inhabitants of Jerusalem; and say to them, 'Thus says the Lord God of Israel: Cursed is the man who does not obey the words of this covenant which I commanded your fathers in the day I brought them out of the land of Egypt, from the iron furnace, saying, Obey My voice, and do according to all that I command you; so shall you be My people, and I will be your God, that I may establish the oath which I have sworn to your fathers, to give them a land flowing with milk and honey, as it is this day.'" And I answered and said, "So be it, Lord" (Jeremiah 11:1-5).

If we obey, we will enjoy His covenant provision and blessing. Are you obedient to the commandments and instructions of God relating to financial prosperity? Are you a faithful and consistent tither? Are you a sacrificial and consistent giver? The way we handle such covenant obligations determines whether we will prosper or not. Many are poor because they live in disobedience to biblical economic principles and wealth creation principles and laws. *If things are tight for you, check your tithe. If you are suffering financially, check your offering.*

CURSES

As we have seen in the previous chapter, poverty is a spirit and a curse. We must address the spiritual dimension of poverty. The spirit realm is where events occur before they happen in the physical; the spirit realm controls the physical realm. Most of the things we see happening in the physical are being manipulated from the spirit realm, and poverty in the lives of many is not an exception. Let's see what Deuteronomy says about curses:

"But it shall come to pass, if you do not obey the voice of the Lord your God, to observe carefully all His commandments and His statutes which I command you today, that all these curses will come upon you and overtake you: Cursed shall you be in the city, and cursed shall you be in the country. Cursed shall be your basket and your kneading bowl. Cursed shall be the fruit of your body and the produce of your land, the increase of your cattle and the offspring of your flocks. Cursed shall you be when you come in, and cursed shall you be when you go out. The Lord will send on you

cursing, confusion, and rebuke in all that you set your hand to do, until you are destroyed and until you perish quickly, because of the wickedness of your doings in which you have forsaken Me" (Deuteronomy 28:15-20).

Mercy, Lord! Can you imagine all that the curse of poverty can cause in people's lives? "Why would a man disobey God and invite all that into his life?" you may ask. The answer is simple: The *spirit* of poverty manipulates a person by making him walk contrary to God's ways and instruction, so that the curse of poverty can be enforced on his life.

The disobedience of man and the sin of Adam brought the curse of poverty upon the entire human race. Lack, hardship, and poverty never existed in the Garden of Eden or in the entire world until man sinned through disobedience.

Then to Adam He said, "Because you have heeded the voice of your wife, and have eaten from the tree of which I commanded you, saying 'You shall not eat of it': Cursed is the ground for your sake; in toil you shall eat of it all the days of your life. Both thorns and thistles it shall bring forth for you, and you shall eat the herb of the field. In the sweat of your face you shall eat bread till you return to the ground, for out of it you were taken; for dust you are, and to dust you shall return" (Genesis 3:17-19).

It took the sacrificial seed of Noah to break the curse upon the ground:

Then Noah built an altar to the Lord, and took of every clean animal and of every clean bird, and offered burnt offerings on the altar. And the Lord smelled a soothing aroma. Then the Lord said in His heart, "I will never again curse the ground for man's sake, although the imagination of man's heart is evil from his youth; nor will I again destroy every living thing as I have done. While the earth remains, seedtime and harvest, cold and heat, winter and summer, and day and night shall not cease" (Genesis 8:20-22).

Noah's seed broke the curse and established an eternal curse-breaking principle called sowing and reaping. God established the principle of sowing and reaping as the way out of the curse of poverty, but disobedience to this law has kept the curse in place. It is the spirit of poverty that can make us:

- stingy toward God and His Kingdom;

- disobedient to God's economic principles;

- unfaithful to God, His Word, and His ways;

- proud and arrogant toward those who try to help us.

The spirit of poverty can make and keep us lazy. It can keep us satisfied with ignorance and away from seeking the information we need for our story to change. Poverty is a curse that must be broken, and it has been through Christ.

> *Christ has redeemed us from the curse of the law, having become a curse for us (for it is written, "Cursed is everyone who hangs on a tree"), that the blessing of Abraham might come upon the Gentiles in Christ Jesus, that we might receive the promise of the Spirit through faith* (Galatians 3:13-14).

Jesus has paid the price for our redemption. When we become covenant children of God, the curse of poverty is rendered powerless over us—unless we invite and permit it back into our lives through *ignorance, unfaithfulness, laziness, pride, sin, disobedience, or curse-inviting habits, attitudes, and lifestyles.*

There is no curse that can prevail without cause. As it says in Proverbs, "Like a flitting sparrow, like a flying swallow, so a curse without cause shall not alight" (Prov. 26:2). Therefore, we should make sure we do not do anything that opens the door for curses to come into our lives so that the work of redemption can be eternally active in us.

Ecclesiastes says, "He that diggeth a pit shall fall into it; and whoso breaketh an hedge, a serpent shall bite him" (Eccles. 10:8 KJV). There is a redemptive hedge around every covenant child of God, but when we break the hedge, we permit the enemy to prevail.

We have examined six universal causes of poverty. Before we examine the final cause of poverty, I want to reemphasize the need to take these truths seriously and make adjustments in your life where necessary. Fight ignorance, resist laziness, shake off unfaithfulness, avoid pride, refuse disobedience, give no room for curses. Do these things and see your story change.

LACK OF AN INVESTMENT MENTALITY

In my travels to other nations, I have observed that—apart from all the other causes of poverty we have examined—this final one seems to be the most rampant. Many do not even realize that lack of an investment mentality is an issue in their lives. Surprisingly, many Christians are poor for this reason alone. This is because while churches have taught extensively on the other causes of poverty, they have failed to address this issue. This lack of instruction may be, in part, due to some church leaders and teachers lacking the knowledge themselves.

Ecclesiastes says, "The labor of fools wearies them, for they do not even know how to go to the city!" (Eccles. 10:15). Some people labor in vain because they do not know how to develop an investment mentality or apply investment principles to get the best return from their labor. In the next chapter, we will look at what keeps people from developing an investment mentality.

Chapter 3

Five Toxic Mentalities

*No one will plan your future for you
if you do not plan it for yourself.*

The lack of an investment mentality has kept many people in the place of poverty, lack, and hardship. Anyone who desires to become rich and wealthy must make a conscious effort to *develop* the mind-set required to make it happen. There are toxic mind-sets that have become prevalent, and these hinder an investment mentality from taking root. In order to develop an investment mentality, we must eradicate toxic mentalities that hinder us. In this chapter, we will look at five toxic mentalities.

NOMADIC MENTALITY

The first toxic mentality that must be eradicated is the nomadic mentality. This reflects a kind of vagabond spirit that controls people. Just as nomads in the physical do not have a fixed location, people with a nomadic mentality move from job to job, place to place, business to business, and church to church without focus or consistency. They lack the staying power to concentrate on one thing until they see results. Nomads are wanderers. They use the resources in one place and then move on to the next. Two major characteristics of nomads are:

- They have no fixed address but wander from place to place.

- They consume all they see and do not plant or produce.

Abraham, the father of faith, came from a nomadic background, but God had to call him out and raise him up in order to change his story. We cannot prosper with a nomadic mentality.

> *Now the Lord had said to Abram: "Get out of your country, from your family and from your father's house, to a land that I will show you. I will make you a great nation; I will bless you and make your name great; and you shall be a blessing. I will bless those who bless you, and I will curse him who curses you; and in you all the families of the earth shall be blessed." So Abram departed as the Lord had spoken to him...* (Genesis 12:1-4).

Abraham had to break free from a nomadic mentality in order to possess the land God promised him. When Abraham arrived in Canaan, God repeated His promise: "Then the Lord appeared to Abram and said, 'To your descendants I will give this land'" (see Gen. 12:7).

Abraham was the first man in the Bible to buy land and pay for it. Even though God had promised Canaan to Abraham, he still had to buy it to activate total possession. Genesis chapter 23 describes how Abraham purchased land as a burial site for his wife, Sarah, after she died in Canaan. First Abraham approached the Hittites and asked them to sell him some property for a burial site (see Gen. 23:4). When they responded favorably, Abraham asked them to approach Ephron on his behalf, so that Ephron would sell Abraham a specific piece of land that he wanted (see Gen. 23:5-9).

Abraham offered to pay full price, but Ephron replied, "No, my lord, hear me: I give you the field and the cave that is in it; I give it to you in the presence of the sons of my people. I give it to you. Bury your dead!" (Gen. 23:11). Abraham again stated that he wanted to pay for the field, and he asked Ephron to accept this (see Gen. 23:12-13). So Ephron set the price, Abraham agreed to the terms, and he purchased the land (see Gen. 23:14-20).

In Genesis chapter 23, we see Abraham paying for land—land that was already promised to him by God. He had a part to play, and he played his part. Just like Abraham, we also have a part to play in order to partake of the wealth transfer agenda of God. The first step is letting go of a nomadic mentality.

CONSUMER MENTALITY

The second toxic mentality that must go is the consumer mentality. To always consume without producing is a great error. Many people spend all their lives consuming everything they can without any provision for savings or investment.

Proverbs tells us, "Be sensible and store up precious treasures—don't waste them like a fool" (Prov. 21:20 CEV). Another version of the same verse says, "There is treasure to be desired and oil in the dwelling of the wise; but a foolish man spendeth it up" (Prov. 21:20 KJV). The New King James version says that a foolish man "squanders it," and the Amplified Bible says he "wastes it" (Prov. 21:20 NKJV, AMP). The New Living Translation states, "The wise have wealth and luxury, but fools spend whatever they get" (Prov. 21:20 NLT). All of these translations emphasize the danger of a consumer mentality. To consume all that you have is foolishness; it closes the door of riches and wealth to you. Many live a prodigal lifestyle of unrestrained spending and end up in shame, poverty, lack, and hardship.

The Book of Genesis describes how Egypt maintained its wealth and survived a time of famine through the wisdom of God that came through Joseph. Joseph counseled Pharaoh against a consumer mentality and enforced a savings and investment culture by asking that 20 percent of all proceeds be saved and reinvested. Joseph said to Pharaoh:

> *Now therefore, let Pharaoh select a discerning and wise man, and set him over the land of Egypt. Let Pharaoh do this, and let him appoint officers over the land, to collect one-fifth of the produce of the land of Egypt in the seven plentiful years. And let them gather all the food of those good years that are coming, and store up grain under the authority of Pharaoh, and let them keep food in the cities. Then that food shall be as a reserve for the land for the seven years of famine which shall be in the land of Egypt, that the land may not perish during the famine* (Genesis 41:33-36).

Today we hear of phrases like "third-world nations" even though God created only one world. Why do you think some nations are classified as third-world? Such nations consume more than they produce, which keeps them at the bottom of the economic ladder because their money exits their economy to pay for importations from producer nations. We must guard against a consumer mentality.

VICTIM OR ENTITLEMENT MENTALITY

The third toxic mentality that needs to be eradicated is the victim or entitlement mentality. This mind-set of always feeling victimized, marginalized, or that someone owes you something must go. No one can make us fail without our permission, so whatever we allow or permit is what we get. Giving excuses and shifting blame are trademarks of this mind-set.

- It's because I'm a woman, or a minority, or an orphan.

- It's because of the devil or my enemies.

- It's because I'm not educated or I'm from a poor family.

Amazingly, for every excuse we give, there are a thousand and one people with worse circumstances who have made it. A victim mentality can keep us in the same spot for life unless we eradicate it.

John chapter 5 provides us with an illustration of victim mentality. Verses 1 through 14 describe the healing of a man at a pool where there were:

> ...sick people, blind, lame, paralyzed, waiting for the moving of the water. For an angel went down at a certain time into the pool and stirred up the water; then whoever stepped in first, after the stirring of the water, was made well of whatever disease he had. Now a certain man was there who had an infirmity thirty-eight years. When Jesus saw him lying there, and knew that he already had been in that condition a long time, He said to him, "Do you want to be made well?" The sick man answered Him, "Sir, I have no man to put me into the pool when the water is stirred up; but while I am coming, another steps down before me." Jesus said to him, "Rise, take up your bed and walk." And immediately the man was made well, took up his bed, and walked... (John 5:3-9).

For thirty-eight years, this man remained in bondage—not because the devil was so powerful or God was powerless, but because his victim mentality kept him bound. A closer look at the story of this man reveals his cooperation with his predicament.

I believe if he were really desperate about his situation, he should have been able to discern the time when an angel came to stir the water. After thirty-eight years of waiting, I do not think that is too much to expect from him. Or why didn't he simply stay in the water and let the angel meet him there when he came? Surely then God would have noticed his desperation and changed his story.

Jesus asked the man a simple question: "Do you want to be made well?" (see John 5:6). The man responded as a victim, making excuses— "while I am coming, another steps down before me" (see John 5:7). His response indicates that even though he knew the opportunity for his freedom was in the pool, he stayed too far away; others were closer to the pool than he was. Why stay far away from what will bless you?

The man's expression "while I am coming," seems to indicate that he could move himself, so why did he also give the excuse that he had "no man to put me into the pool" (see John 5:7)? His response illustrates the victim or entitlement mentality. We should not blame others for what we allow, and we should not expect others to do for us what we are able to do for ourselves.

Finally, if he were really desperate for freedom, why did he settle on the pool as the only option for his freedom? He could have gone to one of Jesus' numerous public gatherings or sought help just like the centurion, Jairus, the woman from Canaan, Bartimaeus, or even the woman with the issue of blood (see Luke 7:1-10; Mark 5:21-24;35-43; Matt. 15:21-28; Mark 10: 46-52; Mark 5:25-34).

A victim or entitlement mentality will keep us in the same place for life unless it is eradicated. We must let go of this mentality.

CIVIL SERVICE, SALARY, OR WAGE MENTALITY

The fourth toxic mentality that must go is the civil service, salary, or wage mentality. Many stay in the poverty zone because they live all their lives expecting their employer, the government, or their salary to make them rich and wealthy. Wake up! None of these are our source— they are only a resource.

It is not an employer's responsibility to make us rich; the responsibility is ours. It is not even the government's responsibility to make us rich. The government should seek to create a favorable environment, an employer should pay salaries, and salaries should become seed for investment and wealth creation. It is not how much we earn that matters, but what we do with what we earn. So, no matter what we are paid, if we do the right things with our salary, we can change our story.

We must move from salary mentality to income mentality. With this shift in mind, we can suddenly grasp the difference between being a salary earner and being an income earner. If you hope to become rich and wealthy through salary alone, you may wait a long time. Only 2 percent of millionaires in the world became so through receiving salaries.

The Difference Between Salaries and Income

What is salary? Salary is fixed. It is set by someone else. It will not increase unless someone else decides to grant a raise. It is the result of labor, and it ceases when you stop working or producing: no work, no pay. It may not be a true reflection of your worth, value, or results. It can be a limitation on your true potential. It can be delayed, withheld, penalized, reduced, or halted by someone else.

What is income? Income is not fixed but can vary over time. It is not determined by someone else. It may come even when you do not labor. It can reflect your true worth, value, and abilities. It can increase exponentially without limits. It is free from the manipulation and oppression of man.

With salary, you work for money. With income, money works for you.

The Story of Esau and Jacob

In Genesis chapter 27, we read about two brothers, Esau and Jacob. When Isaac, their father, was old and his eyes were failing, he called for his oldest son, Esau.

> Then he said, "Behold now, I am old. I do not know the day of my death. Now therefore, please take your weapons, your quiver and your bow, and go out to the field and hunt game for me. And make

*me savory food, such as I love, and bring it to me that I may eat,
that my soul may bless you before I die"* (Genesis 27:2-4).

Rebekah, their mother, overheard this conversation. She favored her younger son, Jacob, and conspired to help him receive the blessing.

*So Rebekah spoke to Jacob her son, saying, "Indeed I heard your
father speak to Esau your brother, saying, 'Bring me game and
make savory food for me, that I may eat it and bless you in the
presence of the Lord before my death.' Now therefore, my son, obey
my voice according to what I command you. Go now to the flock
and bring me from there two choice kids of the goats, and I will
make savory food from them for your father, such as he loves. Then
you shall take it to your father, that he may eat it, and that he
may bless you before his death"* (Genesis 27:6-10).

In this story, Esau is like a salary earner; he needs to hunt to eat. He is an example of hard work and muscle power, which may be slow in producing results. However, Jacob is like an income earner who has a business. An investment or wealth creation system is in place. Read the remaining verses of Genesis chapter 27 to see the triumph and advantage of smart work over hard work, brainpower over muscle power, and income over salary. What Esau went to hunt and labor to get, Jacob reared in the backyard.

The Story of Jacob and Laban

The income and investment mentality, that gave Jacob an edge over Esau also gave him victory over Laban. Jacob refused to remain under the bondage of a salary mentality even though he subjected himself to it for a while.

We read in Genesis that Jacob agreed to work for seven years in order to marry Laban's daughter, Rachel (see Gen. 29:18). Rachel was barren for many years, but eventually she gave birth to a son, Joseph (see Gen. 30:22-24). After Joseph was born, Jacob wanted to quit working for Laban and to establish his own place.

*And it came to pass, when Rachel had borne Joseph, that Jacob
said to Laban, "Send me away, that I may go to my own place and
to my country. Give me my wives and my children for whom I have*

served you, and let me go; for you know my service which I have done for you"(Genesis 30:25-26).

Laban tried to get Jacob to stay by offering him more money, but Jacob wanted to focus on building his own household. Then Laban asked what he should give Jacob in recognition of how his livestock had increased greatly under Jacob's care and so that Jacob could build up his own wealth. They agreed to terms, but then Laban tried to cheat Jacob (see Gen. 30:27-36). In spite of this, Jacob prospered (see Gen. 30:37-43). Genesis says that Jacob "became exceedingly prosperous, and had large flocks, female and male servants, and camels and donkeys" (see Gen. 30:43).

Please read the full story of Jacob and Laban in Genesis chapters 29 through 31 to learn serious lessons about the danger of a life dependent on salary alone. I am not against working for salary, only against anyone seeing salary as their source while excluding an investment mentality. We must let go of a civil service, salary, or wage mentality.

PROSPERITY OR MATERIALISM MENTALITY

The final toxic mind-set that has to be dealt with is the prosperity or materialism mentality. You should know by now that I am not against prosperity, but much of what is taught and labeled "prosperity" today is nothing but materialism and self-centeredness. If your only reason for wanting to be rich and wealthy is so that you can acquire material possessions and get comfort for yourself alone, then your mind-set is wrong. You must move from prosperity-mindedness to posterity-mindedness, with a desire to use your wealth not only to positively affect your generation but also to leave a legacy for future generations.

The five toxic mentalities we have examined in this chapter must be fully eradicated in order to make room for the development of an investment mentality.

Chapter 4

Developing an Investment Mentality

An investment mentality is concerned about the multiplication of all that one has, the acquisition of assets over liabilities, and getting to a place in life where money works for you instead of you working for money.

Having discussed toxic mentalities, it is now time to look at what an investment mentality is. We need to have a clear understanding of what an investment mentality really is, in order to be able to develop it.

Before defining an investment mentality, I want to define some other vital terms:

- *Mentality* is defined as "a mind-set, thought pattern, perception, paradigm, or a way of thinking."

- *Posterity* means "what proceeds from you to your descendants or succeeding generations."

- *Legacy* refers to "something left by will to the next generation."

- *Investment* is "a vehicle or channel, structure, system, or asset that helps in the accumulation and multiplication of money, from time to time, without stress or any addition to the original input." It can be tangible like real estate or businesses; it can also be intangible like stocks, bonds, money markets, etc.

- *Asset* includes "anything you acquire that continues to increase in value or brings continual income to you."

- *Liability* means "anything you acquire that continues to decrease in value or takes money away from you for maintenance and upkeep." Some categorize liabilities as depreciating assets or necessary liabilities.

INVESTMENT MENTALITY DEFINED

What is an investment mentality? It is a mind-set that is concerned about the *multiplication of all that one has.* When we have an investment mentality we are always looking for avenues to multiply what we have through different investment vehicles, rather than consuming or wasting it.

An investment mentality is concerned about the *acquisition of assets over liabilities.* If we have an investment mentality we will be careful about what we do with our money. This means that anytime we spend money, we should try to make sure it is for the acquisition of an asset and not for covering a liability.

An investment mentality is concerned about *getting to a place in life where money works for you* instead of you working for money. If we have an investment mentality, we may start out working for money, but we will have a plan and strategy in place to change our status—to come to a level of financial independence where we no longer work for money but have put money to work on our behalf.

This is what this book is all about. It is a tool to help develop this mind-set, to help discover how to put money to work and become financially free. How do you develop an investment mentality? It's simple. Eradicate the toxic mentalities, learn what an investment mentality is, and make a decision to adjust your mind-set from a toxic to an investment mentality. It is as simple as that—*just make the decision to make adjustments.*

How do you know if you have developed an investment mentality? Consider these two questions:

- What have I been doing with my money up till now?

- What will I do with my money next?

THREE THINGS PEOPLE DO WITH MONEY

There are only three things everyone does with money: waste it, spend it, or invest it. Looking at how we fit under each category can help us determine whether we are still operating with a toxic mind-set or an investment mind-set.

Waste It

One of the things people do with money is waste it; this is what foolish people do. They riotously spend all they have, like the prodigal son. They may work and work but have nothing to show for it because everything they make is wasted on liabilities and perishables. The spirit of poverty can lead to wasting. It manipulates people's minds and makes them impulsively acquire things they do not really want or need. It often motivates impulse and emotional purchases.

Some time ago, I taught on "Freedom from the Spirit of Waste" and revealed how the spirit of poverty makes people waste time, opportunities, relationships, health, lives, and resources. After the service, a lady came to me and asked for prayer against that spirit. I asked her why she thought she needed that freedom, and she revealed to me that she buys three to four new clothing items every month and then does not even wear them. It was July, and she already had over twenty new items that she had bought but never worn that year. I asked her some simple investment questions:

- Do you have a plot of land, a house, or other real estate investment?

- Do you have a portfolio of shares, bonds, etc.?

- Do you have any fixed deposits or savings?

- Do you own a car?

To all these questions she answered no! I counseled her, prayed for her, and gave her some assignments. Today, that same woman is an international businesswoman with her own business, investment portfolio, and real estate holdings. She is a millionaire today because she broke free from waste and became an investor.

The spirit of poverty works in people's lives through three channels, which I call "povertrinity":

- The *waster* is the force behind every form of waste.

- The *devourer* is the force behind every unexpected expense that comes to devour our resources.

- The *emptier* is the force behind every tragedy and calamity that empties or depletes all the fruit of our labor.

Are you a waster? If so, it is time to change. I have seen people waste five years' worth of savings on a one-day wedding ceremony. I have seen people waste huge resources on the naming ceremony of "child number four" even though they were renting a one-room place. I have seen people waste money on clothes, shoes, jewelry, electronic gadgets, handsets, and so on, even though they had no single plot of land to their name.

I have seen waste in many people's lives. I have seen people justify waste, celebrate waste, and enjoy waste only to end up in shame. Thoughts like, "What will people say?" and "How will people feel?" have kept many in wasteland. If we want to become rich and wealthy, we must rise above being manipulated and influenced by people's opinions and status symbols.

When I got married, I did not print wedding invitations, I did not buy or wear a new suit, I did not even have a reception—sounds strange, doesn't it? All the money that could have been spent on such things was instead well-invested in something that will have a lifetime value both for my generation and the next.

Don't be a waster; that is what fools are with money. If you realize that you have been a waster, change now and adopt an investment mentality. Here are some tips for putting wisdom above waste:

- Never allow any form of waste in your life—this includes food, money, time, opportunities, and other resources.

- Never buy what you do not need; purchase only what really needed.

- Never spend money in haste; always think before you spend.

- Never put money into something you have not investigated.

- Always balance emotions with divine leading; avoid impulse buying.
- Always use money with a vision and purpose in mind.

Spend It

The second thing people do with money is spend it. This is what most people do all over the world: they make money, spend it all on bills and necessary liabilities, and start looking for money again. This is why it is called a *rat race*—it is an evil cycle that keeps people trapped. Many people have no savings or investments in place because of this poverty cycle. The reason they give for not being able to save or invest is bills, bills, and more bills.

Here is how most people handle money: First, they acquire money. Next, they spend it on bills and other necessities. After that, they try to save and invest, if they have anything left. Finally, they may try to give something to God. If you are thinking and operating like this without any plan to change, you may never become rich and wealthy.

MAKE MONEY - SPEND IT ON BILLS

The Poverty Cycle of
the Average Man

SPEND IT ON BILLS - MAKE MONEY

To break free from this cycle of poverty—a life of ever spending and never investing—we must embrace a reverse mentality, which is the investment mentality we have been talking about.

Here is how we should handle money: First, we should acquire money. Next, we should settle with God. This means giving a minimum of 10 percent of all income to Him. After that, we should set aside savings and investments. This should be 10 to 20 percent of our income. Finally, we can spend what remains, approximately 70 percent of our income.

If you think this is impossible, think again. We must avoid trying to keep up with the Joneses, and we must seek to live within our means.

Think about how you always find a way to pay bills. This bill-paying ability is all we need to change our story. We simply need to include God and our future (savings, investments) in our bills. Pay God and ourselves (our future) first, and live on the rest. If the 20 to 30 percent we should set aside for God and our future were a new bill that the government imposed, we would find a way to pay it. So consider it a bill to secure your future!

Are you a spender? If so, I encourage you to change the cycle and get out of the rat race. Here are some guidelines for wise spending. Next time, before you spend, ask yourself these questions: Do I really need it? Is the price right? Is the timing right? Is there a better substitute for it? Is there a disadvantage to buying it? Have I researched the item? Will its value increase? Will it require expensive upkeep? Have I compared prices? Is my spouse in agreement? Will I still want this as badly next week, next month, or next year as I do today? Will this purchase improve the quality of my life? Is this purchase within my budget and affordable based on my present financial condition? Will this purchase complement my Christian testimony? Will it help me to achieve God's goals and purposes for my life? These are the kinds of questions we should ask before we spend.

Invest It

The third option for what people do with money is what only a few do. Many waste money, many spend money, but only a few invest money. Fools waste money, most people spend money, but wise people invest money.

One way to tell that you have eradicated toxic mentalities and have developed an investment mentality is if you no longer live life wasting or spending alone, but you are primarily into investing money.

Now that we have looked at what an investment mentality is and what we can do with money, it is time to consider what factors can shape and influence our mentality. This will be the topic of the next chapter.

Chapter 5

Mentality Shapers

*Don't settle for less, for those ahead of you
may be tired of the bondage and hoping
you will be the deliverer.*

Many find it difficult to develop an investment mentality and practice wealth creation principles because they do not understand the factors that affect their mentality. It is time to consider these issues.

UPBRINGING AND FAMILY BACKGROUND

Many people stay at the bottom of life's ladder because they refuse to divorce themselves from things they have picked up and operate by based on their upbringing and background. We may come from a negative background, or we may have had a terrible upbringing—and those definitely contribute to shaping the kind of mentality we have—but we must never allow our background to hinder our higher ground.

> *"What do you mean when you use this proverb concerning the land of Israel, saying: 'The fathers have eaten sour grapes, and the children's teeth are set on edge'? As I live, says the Lord God, you shall no longer use this proverb in Israel"* (Ezekiel 18:2-3).

These verses are saying that we shall not follow the evil pattern of our father's house. We can break free from the collective captivity of our background, separate ourselves from evil inheritance, and plug into God. We see this in the story of Gideon:

Now it came to pass the same night that the Lord said to him "Take your father's young bull, the second bull of seven years old, and tear down the altar of Baal that your father has, and cut down the wooden image that is beside it; and build an altar to the Lord your God on top of this rock in the proper arrangement, and take the second bull and offer a burnt sacrifice with the wood of the image which you shall cut down." So Gideon took ten men from among his servants and did as the Lord had said to him. But because he feared his father's household and the men of the city too much to do it by day, he did it by night. And when the men of the city arose early in the morning, there was the altar of Baal, torn down; and the wooden image that was beside it was cut down, and the second bull was being offered on the altar which had been built. So they said to one another, "Who has done this thing?" And when they had inquired and asked, they said, "Gideon the son of Joash has done this thing." Then the men of the city said to Joash, "Bring out your son, that he may die, because he has torn down the altar of Baal, and because he has cut down the wooden image that was beside it." But Joash said to all who stood against him, "Would you plead for Baal? Would you save him? Let the one who would plead for him be put to death by morning! If he is a god, let him plead for himself, because his altar has been torn down!" Therefore on that day he called him Jerubbaal, saying, "Let Baal plead against him, because he has torn down his altar" (Judges 6:25-32).

It is time to pull down every mental stronghold that has been erected in our minds as a result of our upbringing or background. Gideon had to deal with the altars of his father's house in order to enter into his destiny.

In the Book of Judges, we read that Gideon asked, "O my Lord, how can I save Israel? Indeed my clan is the weakest in Manasseh, and I am the least in my father's house" (see Judg. 6:15). This verse reveals the effect of Gideon's background on his mentality and how it almost robbed him of his destiny. God had to instruct Gideon to destroy the physical altar that enforced the mental stronghold. Did you notice how Gideon's father defended him? (See Judges 6:30-31.) This shows that even Gideon's father was tired and seeking a way out, but he did not have the courage to find it. Don't settle for less, for those ahead of you may be tired of the bondage and hoping you will be the deliverer.

ENVIRONMENT

A second factor that shapes our mentality is environment. Our environment has a lot to do with our mentality and progress in life.

- Where we live matters.

- Where we work matters.

- Where we worship matters.

When a shark is kept in an aquarium, its growth is limited by its environment. But if the same shark is released into the ocean, it then can grow to its full potential. Even the Bible supports the concept that a change of environment can lead to a change in mentality. For 75 years, Abraham's destiny was limited by his environment (see Gen. 12:1-4). Due to his environment:

- He was disconnected from faith in God.

- He was childless after years of marriage.

- He was living below the plan and purpose of God.

- He was operating below his full potential.

- He was a local champion instead of a world changer.

In order for God to use Abraham, to bless him, and to make him a blessing, God had to move him out of his environment to upgrade his mentality. Abraham needed a physical change of environment, but for some of us, we just need to grow beyond our environment so that instead of the environment affecting our mentality, we affect our locality from a higher level.

A few years later, when Abraham's mentality was being corrupted, God brought him out again and lifted him above his environment:

After these things the word of the Lord came to Abram in a vision, saying, "Do not be afraid, Abram. I am your shield, your exceedingly great reward." But Abram said, "Lord God, what will You give me, seeing I go childless, and the heir of my house is Eliezer of Damascus?" Then Abram said, "Look, You have given me no offspring; indeed one born in my house is my heir!" And behold, the word of the Lord came to him, saying, "This one shall not be your heir, but one who will come from your own body shall be your heir." Then He brought him outside and said, "Look now toward heaven, and count the stars if you are able to number them." And He said to him, "So shall your descendants be." And he believed the Lord, and He accounted it to him for righteous-ness (Genesis 15:1-6).

God told Abraham to look toward Heaven so that his perception and mind-set could be upgraded. We must not allow our environment to limit our destiny.

EXPOSURE

The third factor that affects and shapes our mentality is our level of exposure. Many people are born, live, and die in one region of their nation. They never experience the breadth of other cultures and lands. Lack of exposure can lead to a primitive, myopic, warped view of the world and life in general.

The Book of Proverbs instructs us, "Wisdom is the principal thing; therefore get wisdom. And in all your getting, get understanding" (Prov. 4:7). The New Living Translation says, "Getting wisdom is the wisest thing you can do! And whatever else you do, develop good judgment" (Prov. 4:7 NLT).

We should do all we can to develop wisdom, understanding, and good judgment in areas where we lack it. Traveling, excursions, books, tapes, magazines, videos, documentaries, biographies, networking, and so on are all things that can help us gain exposure. We should consider carefully what we expose ourselves to and avoid exposure to anything that may pollute our destiny. As Proverbs says, "Buy the truth, and do not sell it, also wisdom and instruction and understanding" (Prov. 23:23).

Consider the following questions: When did you last read a book? When did you last go on an excursion? When did you last take a trip out of your local area? When did you last experience something new and beneficial? We must not allow lack of exposure to deprive us of our future.

ASSOCIATIONS OR RELATIONSHIPS

I once heard a story about a farmer who stumbled upon the eggs of an eagle while he was on a mountain. The farmer returned to his farm with one of the eagle eggs. He placed the egg among chicken eggs for his chicken to brood with the other eggs. After a while, an eaglet was born and lived with all the chickens on the farm.

He lived where they lived; he did what they did; he feared what they feared. He ate what they ate; he behaved the way they behaved; he suffered what they suffered. But the more the eaglet grew, the more he noticed some differences between himself and the other chicks.

One day he heard the cry of a mother eagle, and something rose up within him. He spread his wings, surrendered to the wind, and soared away into the sky. From day one, the eaglet had the potential to fly and reign in majesty, but his association with chickens limited him and shaped his mentality until he broke free.

You cannot sleep on the lap of Delilah and wake up at the bosom of Abraham. As it says in First Corinthians, "Do not be deceived: 'Evil company corrupts good habits'" (1 Cor. 15:33). Our associations affect our location and our destination in life. It is deceptive to think we can have evil associations and end up in a good destination. Show me your friends, and I will show you the kind of person you are, because as the saying goes, "Birds of a feather flock together."

Proverbs warns us, "He who walks with wise men will be wise, but the companion of fools will be destroyed" (Prov. 13:20). Our associations affect our mentality and determine our destiny. We must be wise and choose our friends with care. We must not allow our associations to hinder our exaltation.

VISION

I once heard another story about a man who was jogging around a lake where people came to fish. After a few laps, he noticed one man who was fishing with a short rod in his hand. Each time he caught a fish, the man held the fish up to the rod and then either put the fish in his basket or threw it back into the water. Out of curiosity, the jogger walked up to the fisherman and asked "Sir, what is the rationale behind your actions? Why do you catch a fish and then throw it back into the water?"

The reply surprised the jogger. The fisherman said, "The rod in my hand is the size of my frying pan, which I measured before leaving home. What I do is simple. Any fish I catch that is longer than the rod will not fit into my frying pan, so I throw it back into the water. However, I keep any fish that is shorter than the length of the rod because I know it will fit into my frying pan." Isn't that amazing! If your frying pan is too small, why not get a bigger one instead of limiting your destiny by the size of your frying pan?

Sometimes we are just like that fisherman. Our vision is too small to accommodate the great things God has in store for us, so we throw away opportunities and limit ourselves with our micro-vision. Dream big to become big because we serve a big God.

The Book of Proverbs warns us, "Where there is no vision, the people perish: but he that keepeth the law, happy is he" (Prov. 29:18 KJV). The Contemporary English Version translates this verse as, "Without guidance from God law and order disappear, but God blesses everyone who obeys His Law" (Prov. 29:18 CEV). The New King James Version says, "Where there is no revelation, the people cast off restraint," and the New Living Translation says, "When people do not accept divine guidance, they run wild" (see Prov. 29:18 NKJV; NLT).

All of these translations tell us that without vision, guidance, and revelation we will run wild, cast off restraint, and perish. We must obey God's law to be happy, joyful, and blessed. We must not allow our vision to limit our provision.

GOD'S WORD

Another powerful mentality shaper is the Word of God. I have seen nobodies become somebodies as a result of an encounter with the Word of God. I am a testimony of what God's Word can do in the mind and life of a man. When I gave God's Word a place in my heart, God gave me a place on earth.

The Bible says we are to "Study to shew thyself approved unto God, a workman that needeth not to be ashamed, rightly dividing the word of truth" (2 Tim. 2:15 KJV). There are three things I do regularly, and I have done them consistently for over fifteen years:

- I read through the Bible once every year.
- I read through Proverbs each month, reading one chapter per day.
- I read an average of one book per week.

Today the wisdom of God is one of my greatest assets due to this discipline. I encourage you to take time for God's Word and let it work wonders in your mind and in your life. We can change our world with the Word of God.

> *In the beginning was the Word, and the Word was with God, and the Word was God. He was in the beginning with God. All things were made through Him, and without Him nothing was made that was made. In Him was life, and the life was the light of men. And the light shines in the darkness, and the darkness did not comprehend it* (John 1:1-5).

THE HOLY SPIRIT—THE ANOINTING

The final mentality shaper is the Holy Spirit, or the anointing of God coming upon our lives. To illustrate this point, I want to tell you the story of an unusual auction.

Once there was a special auction where many people had gathered. The auctioneer picked up a dirty, rickety-looking, old violin as the first item to be auctioned. He started the bidding at 100 dollars, but something strange happened. People started pricing it down instead of up. Someone called for sixty dollars, another, forty, and the offers continued to drop.

The drama continued until an elderly man stood up and walked toward the stage when the bid stood at twenty dollars. This man collected the violin from the auctioneer, dusted it, adjusted it, tuned it, played a little, adjusted and tuned it again, and then began to play. As beautiful music filled the room, everyone was awestruck by the potential in the violin.

After the man finished playing, he handed the violin to the auctioneer and returned to his seat without saying a word. The auctioneer restarted the bidding at 1,000 dollars. That night, the violin sold for over 10,000 dollars. What made the difference? It was the touch of a master's hand and his ability to bring out the best of the violin, revealing its hidden potential for all to see.

Many of us are like that violin, with mentalities that cheapen us and keep us devalued. But when we allow the Holy Spirit to touch us and release His anointing upon us, our mentality will change, our value will increase, and our potential will be maximized.

Another discipline I have cultivated that can help shape mentality is this: I pray in the Holy Spirit for a minimum of one hour every day. Praying in the Holy Spirit helps us operate in the mind of Christ; it reforms our mentality.

Now that we have looked at what shapes our mentality, it is time to consider how God gives us power to get wealth. This will be the topic of the next chapter.

Chapter 6

The Power to Get Wealth

There is much potential buried within us, but
sometimes in life we all need a push.

There once was the story of a very wealthy man, who had an only daughter of marriageable age. One day he made an announcement that any eligible bachelor who wanted the hand of his daughter in marriage should come to his estate for a special contest. On the designated day, hundreds of men from throughout the region gathered, ready to be the lucky one.

Then the wealthy man addressed the crowd: "Welcome, young men. I have a little assignment for all of you, and whoever passes the test will not only have the hand of my daughter in marriage but will also receive a million dollars. Come with me, please."

They all followed him to an Olympic-sized swimming pool. As he threw fresh meat into the water, many alligators came to the surface to feast. The man continued, "The first man to swim across the pool will be the winner."

At this point, over half the men left in anger, calling the wealthy man a wicked murderer. Others were still standing around the pool, weighing their options and speaking with one another. Suddenly, everyone heard a splash! They saw one man in the pool, swimming hard to escape the alligators and reach the other side. Everyone was shocked! Before they could react, the man was out on the other side of the pool, gasping for air.

Everyone, including the wealthy man, rushed to meet him. With a look of surprise, the wealthy man said, "Congratulations, young man! You amaze me—I never expected anyone to go to such lengths to have my daughter. You have proven yourself. Come with me to receive your reward and discuss marriage plans."

The young man—still panting heavily—spoke in anger, "I do not need your money, and I do not want your daughter. All I want to know is, *who pushed me* into the pool?"

Whoa! *Who pushed him?* He did not go in willingly; someone accidentally or deliberately pushed him in. Whether he was accidentally or intentionally pushed, he made it. If he had not been pushed, he would never have believed he could make it.

The young man in this story illustrates how there is much potential buried within us that lies dormant. Perhaps we have not allowed our potential to find expression. Sometimes in life we all need a push. This book is meant to push you into the place of wealth.

A Common Misunderstanding About Wealth

There is a common error in teachings on the power to get wealth that I want to deal with in this chapter. This is vital because the error has become a tool to bring poverty to the Church. The root of this teaching is from Deuteronomy:

> *"And you shall remember the Lord your God, for it is He who gives you power to get wealth, that He may establish His covenant which He swore to your fathers, as it is this day"* (Deuteronomy 8:18).

I have seen many use this verse as a basis to pray for God to give them wealth. I have read this verse—and the entire chapter of Deuteronomy 8—numerous times, and I wonder why I do not see what others see. Many pray for God to give them wealth, but I wonder why people pray a prayer that is exactly the opposite of what this verse reveals. God does not give wealth; He gives the power to create wealth.

God gives us power—that is, ability and empowerment—to get or create wealth. It is God's responsibility to give us power, but it is our responsibility to use the power to create wealth. Three vital truths are revealed in this one verse that we must realize if we ever want to become rich and wealthy:

- God does not give wealth; He only gives the power to get or create wealth.

- Until we use the power we have been given to create wealth, we will remain empowered but poor.

- Establishing God's covenant is the primary purpose for wealth.

Proverbs tells us, "The blessing of the Lord makes one rich, and He adds no sorrow with it" (Prov. 10:22). The blessing of the Lord *makes*, that is, produces or creates riches when utilized. The Hebrew word that is translated as "power" in Deuteronomy 8:18 is the same word that is translated as "blessing" in Proverbs 10:22. The Lord gives us power and blessing, but we need to use them to create wealth.

UNVEILING THE POWER

When people hear teaching about the power of wealth, they are often confused about what this power is. Some people think it means having a spiritual cloud upon them. What is the "power to get wealth" that God has given His covenant children? Ignorance of this power has kept many confused and frustrated.

For many years, I was like other Christians, confused and frustrated because I believed that God's Word said I had been given power to get wealth, but I could not see wealth. I sought God, and He gave me insight into what the power really means. When God said He gives power to get wealth, He was referring to seven vital ingredients by this one word. Let's look at each in turn.

KNOWLEDGE AND INFORMATION

My people are destroyed for lack of knowledge. Because you have rejected knowledge, I also will reject you from being priest for Me; because you have forgotten the law of your God, I also will forget your children (Hosea 4:6).

One thing God meant when He said that He gives us power to get wealth is that He gives us knowledge and information to get or create wealth. We should seek knowledge and information from God's Word—and from other sources such as books, tapes, CDs, and so on—so that we can be better equipped to create wealth.

As I mentioned earlier, ignorance is one of the universal causes of poverty. When we obtain knowledge and information, we have what it takes to deal with poverty. God can provide food for us, but God cannot eat the food on our behalf. God has provided all the information we need to create wealth; it is all around us in different formats. But we have the responsibility to receive this information and knowledge and use it.

OPPORTUNITIES

Whatever your hand finds to do, do it with your might; for there is no work or device or knowledge or wisdom in the grave where you are going. I returned and saw under the sun that—the race is not to the swift, nor the battle to the strong, nor bread to the wise, nor riches to men of understanding, nor favor to men of skill; but time and chance happen to them all. For man also does not know his time: like fish taken in a cruel net, like birds caught in a snare, so the sons of men are snared in an evil time, when it falls suddenly upon them (Ecclesiastes 9:10-12).

Another thing God meant when He said that He gives us power to get wealth is that He has given us opportunities to create wealth. Opportunities include open doors, contacts, circumstances, and ladders that bring promotion. Whatever your hand finds to do, do it, because time and chance have been given to you. All the opportunities that come our way are God's power for us to create wealth.

Opportunity plus preparation leads to success. But if an opportunity comes when you are unprepared, you may miss it. Many people do not know how to identify opportunities when they come, so they miss them. What is an opportunity?

- Meeting people is an opportunity.

- Reading a book is an opportunity.

- Visiting someplace is an opportunity.

- Giving is an opportunity.

- Doing something is an opportunity.

- Leading or coordinating is an opportunity.

- Working someplace is an opportunity.

- Worshiping someplace is an opportunity.

- Attending a seminar or training is an opportunity.

- Having an idea or product is an opportunity.

- Discovering a problem is an opportunity.

- Identifying a need is an opportunity.

There are opportunities everywhere. All you need to do is look a little closer. To gain greater understanding of opportunity, I encourage you to read my book entitled *Maximizing Opportunity*.

CHOICE

See, I have set before you today life and good, death and evil.... I call heaven and earth as witnesses today against you, that I have set before you life and death, blessing and cursing; therefore choose life, that both you and your descendants may live (Deuteronomy 30:15,19).

The next thing meant by power to get wealth is choice. God has created all mankind as free moral agents with the liberty to choose. He sets before everyone both negative and positive possibilities, while advising us to choose good instead of evil.

Have you noticed that where you are today is a result of the choices you made yesterday, and where you will be tomorrow will be determined by the choices you make today? The ability to choose is a power we have been given to create wealth because it helps us decide what to do, what not to do, and how to plan for our future. Whether we make it in life or not is really our choice.

GIFTS, TALENTS, AND POTENTIAL

Now to Him who is able to do exceedingly abundantly above all that we ask or think, according to the power that works in us (Ephesians 3:20).

Another aspect of the power that God has given us to create wealth is the gifts, talents, and potential He has put within us. God put these in us, but it is up to us to use them. As it has been said, our wealth is tied to our talent, our gold is tied to our gifts, our profit is tied to our potential, and our wealth is tied to our "well" within.

There is a power at work in us that can produce beyond our wildest thoughts and imaginations. We only need to discover the power and put it to work. We need to:

- discover our gifts, talents, and potential;

- develop them consistently to become skillful;

- declare and deploy them to create wealth.

We must not ignore the gifts, talents, and potential we have, because they are the power God gives to create wealth.

THE WORD OF GOD

All Scripture is given by inspiration of God, and is profitable for doctrine, for reproof, for correction, for instruction in righteousness, that the man of God may be complete, thoroughly equipped for every good work (2 Timothy 3:16-17).

We cannot give God's Word a place in our life and end up in shame. God's Word empowers us for wealth creation in several ways:

- It helps us to know God and His ways.

- It helps us to understand the devil and his ways.

- It helps us to understand life and its ways.

God's Word fully equips us to win in life, because it gives us leverage in life. When God said, "I give you power to get wealth," His Word was one of power. Colossians instructs us:

72

Let the word of Christ dwell in you richly in all wisdom, teaching and admonishing one another in psalms and hymns and spiritual songs, singing with grace in your hearts to the Lord. And whatever you do in word or deed, do all in the name of the Lord Jesus, giving thanks to God the Father through Him (Colossians 3:16-17).

PRAYER

Now Jabez was more honorable than his brothers, and his mother called his name Jabez, saying, "Because I bore him in pain." And Jabez called on the God of Israel saying, "Oh, that You would bless me indeed, and enlarge my territory, that Your hand would be with me, and that You would keep me from evil, that I may not cause pain!" So God granted him what he requested (1 Chronicles 4:9-10).

Prayer changes things, prayer moves the hand that moves the world, and prayer makes power available for wealth creation. One aspect of the power to get wealth is the power of prayer.

Prayer helps to change situations in our favor. Prayer helps to move God to act on our behalf. Prayer helps to put the devil and his host where they belong. Prayer helps to make impossibilities become possible. Prayer helps to create supernatural wealth. To ignore prayer is to ignore a major power for wealth creation. In the Book of Luke, we read what happened when Jesus prayed:

When all the people were baptized, it came to pass that Jesus also was baptized; and while He prayed, the heaven was opened. And the Holy Spirit descended in bodily form like a dove upon Him, and a voice came from heaven which said, "You are My beloved Son; in You I am well pleased" (Luke 3:21-22).

When Jesus prayed at His baptism, Heaven opened over Him. Prayer makes Heaven open over our heads, and when we operate under open heavens, we cannot end in poverty.

THE ANOINTING

It shall come to pass in that day that his burden will be taken away from your shoulder, and his yoke from your neck, and the yoke will be destroyed because of the anointing oil (Isaiah 10:27).

The final aspect to the power God has given us to get wealth is the anointing. The anointing is the hand of God upon man. It is the presence of God upon man. It is the burden-removing, yoke-destroying power of God. It is the tangible presence of the Holy Spirit in our lives. It is the wisdom imparter and idea generator.

Wisdom and ideas for wealth creation flow when the anointing comes or resides upon us. It is like the violin in the story we read earlier. When the anointing comes, our lives take a turn for the better. The anointing makes the difference; it baptizes us with favor. When God said, "I have given you power to get wealth," He also meant the anointing to create wealth.

THE EMMANUEL TRANSLATION

I hope this chapter has provided a better understanding of what the "power to get wealth" really means. It goes beyond all the spiritual and religious razzmatazz we may have assumed it to mean. When I grasped this revelation, it changed everything—and I believe it will work for you, too. Here is my translation of Deuteronomy chapter 8 verse 18:

And you shall remember the Lord your God, for it is He who gives you the power (that is, the knowledge, opportunity, choice, potential, gifts, talents, Word, prayer, and anointing) to create wealth on earth so that you can use the wealth to establish His Kingdom and covenant on earth as He has covenanted with those who have gone before us (author's paraphrase).

Having come this far, it is time for us to go deeper and discover the pathway to wealth. It takes an *investment mentality* and a *proper understanding of the power to get wealth* for anyone to be able to discover the pathway to wealth, to take a journey on the pathway, and to successfully arrive a position of wealth. Now that we have discussed those two issues, it is time to look at the pathway to wealth.

Chapter 7

The Pathway to Wealth—
Financial Intelligence

*It is not how much we earn, but what we
do with what we earn that matters.*

The journey to financial freedom is one that everyone who desires to be rich and wealthy must take. However, no one can arrive someplace without knowing the pathway that leads to the destination. The kind of vehicle you use and the speed with which you move is irrelevant if you are on the wrong pathway.

Have you ever taken a bus, train, ship, or plane; enjoyed the trip; and arrived at the other side—only to discover you took the wrong bus, train, ship, or plane to get there? I have seen people do all kinds of things to climb the corporate success ladder, only to get to the top and discover that the ladder was leaning on the wrong wall. In order to arrive at a position of wealth, we must find the pathway that leads to wealth. As it says in Ecclesiastes, "The labor of fools wearies them, for they do not even know how to go to the city!" (Eccles. 10:15).

How do we discover and walk this path that leads to wealth? There are three steps—or better still, three bus stops—on the pathway to wealth. Everyone who desires to arrive at a position of wealth must go through these three steps (or bus stops) without fail, or else they will never reach their destination. Instead they will be consumed in the journey.

The three bus stops are: financial intelligence, financial planning, and financial discipline. In the next three chapters, we will look at each of these important steps to discovering the pathway to wealth.

First Bus Stop—Financial Intelligence

Financial intelligence, which is an investment mentality, is the first step on this pathway. It refers to the power to get wealth and more. Amazingly, many people go to school and graduate without gaining financial intelligence. Many people work in financial institutions and manage other people's money without having financial intelligence.

Going to school will not automatically make one financially intelligent because many schools do not teach about this. I would think that if going to school made one financially intelligent, all professors and graduates would be wealthy.

Financial intelligence involves the understanding of the inner workings of money. It includes comprehending:

- How to make, manage, and multiply money.
- How to create and build wealth with little or no money at all.
- The vehicles of wealth.
- The place of inflation, cash flow, delayed gratification, compound interest, and so on.
- How to develop an investment mentality.
- The power available for wealth creation.
- The difference between assets and liabilities, salaries and income, good debt and bad debt, leverages and bondages, and so on.

Are you financially literate? Financial intelligence does not necessarily come from a formal institution or school. It is a function of re-defined education that comes from personal development through reading books like this; listening to or watching tapes, CDs, and DVDs that reveal and educate; attending training and seminars on relevant issues; networking and developing valuable associations or relationships. Regardless of what we study or do for a living, if we do not have financial intelligence we will not be on the pathway to wealth.

A LOOK AT FORMAL EDUCATION

When I teach about the pathway to wealth, I often say, "If you want to be rich and wealthy, don't go to school." This may sound shocking, but try not to prejudge this revelation until you read further and consider what I am trying to communicate.

Have you ever thought about where and how formal education, schools, and institutions started? There was no school in the Garden of Eden. Everything Adam and Eve learned was from God, by revelation in the cool of the day. God's education comes from revelation, not institutions.

Educational institutes either originate from God—as channels for making God's mind, plans, purposes, and ways clear to man—or they originate from Egypt, where formal institutions and schools as we know them first began. Schools developed in Egypt as a way to teach and pass down ways, traditions, and worship to others. Simply put, education was a way to keep people in bondage to the gods and ways of Egypt.

Looking at present-day schools, I believe that 95 percent of the school systems in the world today have one primary agenda. They are set up to qualify people to get a "good job." This means that by going to school, we are prepared to look for a job rather than to look for a way to create a job. An old Hebrew states, "He that teaches not his son a trade is as if he taught him to be a thief."

A LOOK AT HISTORY

Take a trip with me back into Nigerian history. Before the colonial masters came, our great-grandparents were entrepreneurs. They were hunters, farmers, traders, or manufacturers. This they did, and they raised their children successfully—even with polygamy. Then came the colonial masters. They took the entrepreneurial skills and entrepreneurial system away from us and replaced them with educational institutions and salaried job opportunities. Our great-grandparents took the bait and became captive. We lost our birthright for a morsel of bread.

Parents trained and raised their children to desire colonial education and salaried jobs with retirement benefits instead of raising them to be entrepreneurs as ordained by God. The initial benefits made the deception easy. People attended school; they went to Europe to continue their education; they received good jobs in colonial-controlled and colonial-managed companies. They obtained salaries, cars, bonuses, and travel opportunities, but with all these benefits, they lacked a vital tool for wealth creation: an investment mentality—financial intelligence.

They had no savings and no investments. They had no real estate or assets. They had no companies or businesses of their own. They retired with huge sums of money but no financial intelligence to manage or multiply it, and no entrepreneurial skills to start a new business successfully.

I know people who lived in London in the 1950s, '60s, and '70s but did not buy a single piece of property. They lived in flats and apartments for decades as tenants. They worked and retired, but they were too tired and financially illiterate to be wealthy.

A LOOK AT TODAY

Today, thousands of graduates leave school with various certificates and degrees but also with a great degree of financial illiteracy and entrepreneurial ignorance. Over 70 percent of them remain unemployed after the first two years. Over 50 percent of those who get jobs are underemployed. Many years after graduation, they still go from interview to interview seeking their dream jobs.

It is not unusual to see a great number of graduates respond to a single job vacancy advertisement, even though only one person is needed. I once went to a friend's office and saw over a thousand people waiting. Later, I discovered that my friend had advertised in a national daily for a single vacant position, but over a thousand educated graduates had applied.

It pains my heart to see people today—especially youth who are victims of formal education—moving about helpless and hopeless because they went to school but lack financial intelligence and entrepreneurial skills. No wonder our youth now look for "get-rich-quick schemes" and "escape routes" from their present situation.

And guess what? The colonial system still has ways to take them to the next level of bondage with "visa lotteries" and "special immigration programs." Today our brain drain has become brain gain for other countries.

TIME FOR A REVOLUTION

Our entire educational system needs overhauling. No one should go through school without being taught the practical principles for success, wealth creation, and entrepreneurship.

These concepts should be included in the curriculum from the primary or elementary level to the tertiary level. No one should be allowed to graduate from a higher institution without being schooled in the arts of wealth creation, entrepreneurship, and self-reliance.

If this were done, it would eradicate the present situation—where people graduate with a wealth of theoretical knowledge that is useless to them because they do not know how to apply it in a practical way. It would also reduce crime, violence, and poverty.

A WORD OF BALANCE

The ideas I have shared may sound radical. I want to make it clear that I am not against education, schools, or institutions. I am a graduate myself and have attended various institutions. All I am trying to get across is the limitation of allowing formal education to be your only education, without embracing the redefined education that equips us with what we really need for wealth creation. *If you want to be rich, go to school, but get financial intelligence and develop an investment mentality and entrepreneurial skills to complete it.*

This book is filled with much information that will increase your financial intelligence. However, do not let it be your only resource. I encourage you to make a commitment to prioritize personal development and seek out other materials to gain financial intelligence. This is essential because developing financial intelligence is a continual process. As we embrace financial intelligence, we are already on the pathway that leads to wealth.

Chapter 8

The Pathway to Wealth— Financial Planning

We cannot become financial goal-getters,
unless we are first financial goal-setters.

The second bus stop to financial independence on the pathway to wealth is the need for financial planning. Failure to plan always translates to planning for failure. Jesus validated the place and importance of planning in all we do when He said:

> *"For which of you, intending to build a tower, does not sit down first and count the cost, whether he has enough to finish it—lest, after he has laid the foundation, and is not able to finish, all who see it begin to mock him, saying, 'This man began to build and was not able to finish'? Or what king, going to make war against another king, does not sit down first and consider whether he is able with ten thousand to meet him who comes against him with twenty thousand? Or else, while the other is still a great way off, he sends a delegation and asks conditions of peace"* (Luke 14:28-32).

Proper planning prevents poor performance and determines the result that one gets in any aspect of life. In order to become financially independent and free, one needs financial intelligence and a financial plan to arrive at a place of wealth.

Many people gain financial intelligence but fail to achieve their desired goals because they have no plan in place to actualize their goals. Do not expect to arrive at a level of wealth you have not planned for, because the dream you do not work toward will never become a reality. Financial planning includes the strategy, action steps, and structure that we put in place to achieve a desired goal or objective. We cannot become financial goal-getters, unless we are first financial goal-setters.

STAGES OF LIFE

What is your plan for your future? To help motivate you to create a financial plan, let me share with you about the stages of life. There are three major stages: learning, earning, and turning.

The Learning Stage

The first stage of life is the learning stage. This stage usually encompasses birth through age 25. This is the time when we are expected to learn all the basics of life and get enough qualifications and credentials for the next stage. During this stage:

- We should get connected to God.

- We should mature and gain understanding of the basics of life.

- We should complete our formal education and graduate.

- We should discover our vision and purpose in life.

- We should discover our career or area of focus and get all we need to pursue that career.

- We should be fully set for the next stage.

If at age 25, you do not have a vision or purpose for life, you are still waiting to get admission into a college or university, or you have yet to receive a certificate or diploma or to find a career, then your life is already operating behind schedule and you need to avoid distraction and speed things up.

I have seen people over age 25 still trying to qualify for college or university admission, and yet they think they have all the time in the world. Do not mess up your life or toy with your destiny; get serious and be an achiever. Most importantly, if we reach the end of this stage without knowing God and serving Him, the next stage will be that much harder.

The Earning Stage

The second stage of life—the earning stage—falls between the ages of 25 and 50. This is when we are expected to be earning a living, earning income. During this time, we should be using what we learned in the first stage to earn a living and produce fruit for life.

- We should be living and burning for God at this stage.
- We should be married.
- We should be parents or raising children.
- We should be using financial intelligence to secure our future.
- We should be at our prime and our maximum productivity.

If at this stage, you are still trying to pursue a degree or decide on a career, or if you are taking life for granted and are devoid of an investment mentality, you are operating behind schedule. If you marry at forty, when will you have and raise children? Do you really still want to be changing diapers at sixty and taking children to school?

Consider this: think of how old you were when you had your last child; now add twenty to thirty years to the age you were at that time. That is when you can expect to be free from school fees. Shouldn't that motivate us to wake up, get serious, and have a plan for our future? If we reach the end of this stage without knowing God and living for Him, we are close to having lived a wasted life.

The Turning Stage

The turning stage is the last stage of life. It includes age 50 and older. By this time, we are expected to have gained financial independence and perhaps even retired early. This is the stage where we should be mentoring and impacting the next generation with our wealth of experience.

- We should not be nursing a baby at this stage.
- We should not be looking for a job or career.
- We should not be in school.
- We should not be unmarried.

- We should not be poor.

- We should not be a tenant.

Most importantly, we should not be an enemy of God at this stage, or else we will die and end up in hell, with our life having been a useless existence.

I do not know where you fall in these stages of life, but I hope that you can now see the vital need for having a financial plan to secure your future. There is no security in social security; many nations have trillions of dollars in unpaid pensions, with pensioners living in penury. As I said before, no one will plan your future for you if you do not plan it for yourself. Without a plan in place, poverty will come:

> Go to the ant, you sluggard! Consider her ways and be wise, which, having no captain, overseer or ruler, provides her supplies in the summer, and gathers her food in the harvest. How long will you slumber, O sluggard? When will you rise from your sleep? A little sleep, a little slumber, a little folding of the hands to sleep—so shall your poverty come on you like a prowler, and your need like an armed man (Proverbs 6:6-11).

THREE STEPS TO FINANCIAL PLANNING

Now that we have considered the importance of financial planning by studying the stages of life, it is time to look more closely at what is involved in financial planning. There are *three steps to financial planning* that must be followed: ascertain your location, determine your destination, and choose your vehicle.

Ascertain Your Location

We cannot progress successfully on this pathway and plan well without first finding out our present position. We need to know our present position in order to plot and navigate to our expected destination. How do you ascertain your location? First, consider these questions:

- How old are you now?

- How rich or poor are you now?

- What sources of income do you have now?

84

- What potential income sources are at your disposal?
- Do you presently have an investment mentality and financial intelligence?
- Do you have any investment plan in place?
- Are you in debt now?

Now go back and revisit the Financial Intelligence Questionnaire. This will help you locate your present position. If you are in debt, your first step will be to get out of debt. If you are not in debt but have no source of income, your first step will be to get a source of income. If you have only one source of income, you should explore other sources of income to add to your present level.

How can one get out of debt? First, get connected to God and invite Him to help you. Then, list all your debts and have a clear idea of what you owe. Do not go deeper in debt or add to what you already owe. Start reducing your debt, no matter how small your payments may be. Pay off your debts little by little, one by one, prioritizing and reducing your total debt. Cut expenses and avoid excesses. Get out of debt and stay out. Pray against the spirit of poverty and debt throughout the process.

How do people get money? There are many ways to acquire money, but some ways are not positive and should be avoided. Some people get it by stealing, cheating, or fraud. Others borrow or beg. Still others try lotteries or gambling. Some marry for money, but that is not the purpose of marriage. Inheritance is a more positive way to acquire money, but this is not supposed to be a primary source. A better way is to gain income from business, employment, or salaried jobs.

Have you ascertained your location? Everyone should do this in order to succeed in financial planning. (There is a workbook at the end of this book to help you.) If you have ascertained your location, then it is time to look at the second step.

Determine Your Destination

If we do not know where we are going, how will we know when we get there? If there is no finishing line, we will not know when we finish. If there is no goalpost, we will not know when we score a goal.

Determining your destination before commencing a journey is the normal thing to do. Can you imagine someone leaving home on a journey without any fixed destination in mind? Well, I can imagine it because I have seen it happen many times in people's lives. Many leave their lives to chance without any vision or focus. "Whatever will be will be" is the deceptive philosophy of such a person. If you have ascertained your location and know where you stand, the next thing is to determine your destination. Start by considering these questions:

- When do you want to retire or gain financial independence?

- How old do you want to be when this happens?

- How much will you need to take care of yourself and your obligations or responsibilities then?

- How rich and comfortable do you want to be?

Retirement planning is something we must not leave in the hands of others to manage without our direct involvement. Retirement is the period of time or season of our life when we are out of active service. At this stage, we are expected to have attained financial independence. That means even if we no longer work or make any extra income, the returns from existing investments should be adequate for all our needs, wants, and luxuries without completely depleting our investments.

Research has shown that if you were to randomly select 100 twenty-year-old men and follow them for forty years—until they were sixty—you would see the following result:

- 1 percent will have attained financial independence and become extremely rich and wealthy.

- 4 percent will be rich and wealthy.

- 5 percent will still be working and struggling to make ends meet.

- 36 percent will be dead.

- 54 percent will be broke, poor, penniless, and dependent on relatives, their children, the government, or church welfare.

Now consider where you stand. Have you retired already? If so, which percentile do you fall under? Have you yet to turn sixty or retire?

How much longer do you have, and which percentile will you fall under? Note that none of the outcomes were thrust upon any of the young men. Their outcome was a result of their choices and their planning—or lack of planning.

We all need to have a financial plan for our retirement and for our future. If you have ascertained your location and determined your destination, then you are set for the final step to financial planning.

Choose Your Vehicle

Vehicle is an investment term used to describe "a channel, strategy, or type of investment" one chooses to use. Just like we have in the physical, so it is in the world of investments. To move from point A to point B in the physical, we need a means of transportation or a vehicle. In the physical, possible vehicles include—but are not limited to—legs, a bicycle, motorcycle, train, car, truck, ship, airplane, and so on. The vehicle we choose determines how fast we get from point A to point B, and it also determines whether we will ever arrive—depending on the distance between the two points.

ASCERTAIN YOUR LOCATION	CHOOSE YOUR VEHICLE	DETERMINE YOUR DESTINATION

In the world of investment, there are different investment vehicles available to take us from one point to another. To move from your present location (which I expect you have ascertained by now), to your destination (which I also expect you have determined), you need to have a strategic plan in place for how to achieve your goal. Choosing the right vehicle or investment plan and strategy determines how soon you can achieve your goal.

Possible investment vehicles include: paid employment; stocks or money markets (including savings, fixed deposits, shares, bonds, mutual funds, investment clubs); owning a business (in manufacturing, trade, services, etc.); real estate; intellectual property (developing ideas and products, royalty producers, skills and talents).

In considering investment vehicles, there are several vital things to note:

- How early you start investing matters greatly.

- How much you invest matters.

- What interest or rate of return you get matters.

- How consistent you are in investing matters.

- What you do with your interest and returns matters.

STRATEGIES FOR FINANCIAL PLANNING

Everything we have learned so far comes into play now because, until the information is put into practice, it remains dormant. Let us look into how to practically and strategically apply these truths to achieve our goals.

The first step is to have a steady, consistent source of income. The next step is to apply investment principles to the income you generate. If you are employed, give your best at your job. Be the best worker and make your employer proud—this will help you to gain job security.

Remember, it is not how much we make that matters, but what we do with what we make. One key discipline to adopt is to ensure that we live below our means or spend less than we earn.

The 30:70 Principle

To become rich and wealthy and gain financial independence, we should not spend over 70 percent of our income. This means that 30 percent should always be set aside for God and our future. The income we receive should be distributed as follows:

- Ten percent should go to tithe and charity.

- Ten percent should go to savings and investments.

- Ten percent should go toward personal development.

- Seventy percent should be what we live on.

Regardless of how we receive income—weekly, monthly, or periodically—we should follow this plan.

The first 10 percent of all income should go to God as a tithe. I do not wish to get into a debate or religious argument regarding this point. If you do not believe in tithing, then think of it as 10 percent toward charity, but make sure the first 10 percent of all income goes to God. This serves as an acknowledgement of the fact that He is our source, we appreciate His provision, and we need His guidance, direction, and protection for the remaining 90 percent. What we do with the first 10 percent determines what happens to the other 90 percent.

Of the remaining 90 percent, 10 percent should go toward savings and investment, and 10 percent should go toward personal development. Both of these are forms of investment and saving for our future. Investing in personal development—in order to stay updated and relevant—is vital to maintaining job security and cash flow.

Finally, we should live on 70 percent of what we make. To do this, we should make and follow a budget that includes our bills, needs, and necessities. If you cannot afford or accommodate something within your 70 percent, then it is not for you yet. I encourage you to do all you can to live within your means and follow this plan, no matter how tight it may seem. Remember, this will help you to reach your goals.

A Word on Savings

It is essential to have a bank account if you want to become rich and wealthy. You need to have a savings mind-set to safeguard your future. If you do not have an account, make sure you open one this week; not having a bank account is a sign of having a consumer mentality. If money is not saved or invested:

- you will not be turning it over;
- you will not be earning any interest on it;
- you will be limited by what you can keep on hand;
- you will end up wasting or spending it recklessly without vision, purpose, or planning because it is easily accessible to you.

A Word on Budgeting

Budgeting is a financial planning mechanism you should put in place to help you become financially independent. It is an estimate of all expected income and expenditures over a specific period of time—monthly, quarterly, and annually. It should include all anticipated income, expenditures, assets, liabilities, and cash flow for a specific period. When you have a budget in place, it helps you to make better financial choices among different alternatives. As I mentioned before, expenses should never be allowed to be higher than your income, or else debt and poverty will be the result. Having a proper budget in place helps to ensure that you live within your means.

I can think of seven reasons why everyone needs a budget:

1. It helps you to control your money instead of your money controlling you.

2. It helps you to know whether you are living within your means or above your means.

3. It assists you in your savings and investment goals.

4. It is a guide that tells you whether you are heading toward your desired financial goals.

5. It helps you to prepare for financial emergencies and unexpected expenses that might otherwise destabilize you.

6. It helps to keep you out of debt, and it gets you out of debt if you are already in debt.

7. It helps to reveal areas where you are spending too much money, and it helps you to refocus on more important financial goals.

FIVE VITAL INVESTMENT PRINCIPLES

When considering financial planning, there are five vital investment principles to note: planning, time, inflation, compound interest, and the power of annuity. It is time to discuss these issues.

The Principle of Planning

It is important to take investment planning seriously, because this is what will take you from your present position to your desired destination. Planning enables you to know how wealthy you are, which investment vehicles to use, and how much to set aside on a periodic basis. It also enables you to stay focused and disciplined.

Proper financial planning requires knowing what kind of income you are generating. There are three types of income:

- *Earned income* is generally derived from salaried jobs, paid or contract employment, or some form of labor.

- *Portfolio income* is generally derived from paper assets such as stocks, bonds, mutual funds, and so on.

- *Passive income* is generally derived from real estate or royalties.

Your financial plan should focus on how to convert earned income into portfolio income and passive income as efficiently as possible. This is why between 10 to 20 percent of *all income* you receive should be saved or invested so that it can become portfolio or passive income. Earned income ceases after you retire or when you cannot keep working for health or other reasons. If you have not kept to the 30:70 principle—converting your earned income into passive or portfolio income during your active working years—you will have nothing to fall back on during your retirement years, and, needless to say, you will not be rich, wealthy, or financially independent.

The Principle of Time

Regarding financial planning, it is important to consider the element of time because, as it has been said: time waits for no one, time is money, and time wasted equals money wasted. Remember, it is not how much you invest but how early you start investing that really matters.

Time can either be your enemy or your friend. When you delay acting on what you know, or delay investing, you shorten the amount of time that your money can be put to work. If you wait to start saving or investing, you will then need to make higher returns to meet your goals. If you haven't already, now is the time to start putting all these principles to work. Procrastination and delay can be dangerous. Remember, procrastination is a form of laziness, and it leads to poverty.

Let me pause here to give you a practical example. The Fingerprint Investment Club has been earning a rate of return on investment of 20 percent per year for its members. So if, for example, parents with financial intelligence began investing 5,000 naira per month (or 60,000 naira per year) for their child when he was born, they would have quite a tidy amount after some years. [NOTE: the *naira* (*N* or *NGN*) is the currency of Nigeria.] When their child turned twenty, they would have over 13 million naira invested! How many twenty-year-olds do you know with that kind of nest egg?

But if a man does not start early but invests the same amount as those parents, starting at age forty, he would be sixty years old before he would accumulate the same amount as the child had by age 20.

The parents and the man invested the same amount, over the same period of time, at the same interest rate, but beginning at different ages. The point is, it is good to start early and use time to your advantage. Regardless of where you live, all you need to do is to apply these principles. They can work anywhere in the world.

The Principle of Inflation

Another critical investment principle to consider is how to relate to inflation. Inflation can become a major obstacle to our financial goals if we do not invest above it. Any investment vehicle we choose must be able to exceed the rate of inflation where we live. Allow me to illustrate this point with a few stories.

There once was a man who invested ten dollars in an interest-yielding savings account. Then he fell asleep for a very long time. When he awoke thirty years later, his ten-dollar investment had become 30 million dollars! What a wealthy man, you might think. But before you shout, consider that as he slept for thirty years, inflation rose dramatically. Now his 30 million dollars could only buy a three-minute phone call because, due to inflation, calls now cost 1 million dollars per minute!

Now let's consider a story of the naira, the currency of Nigeria. Think if you were to invest 10,000 naira per year and gain 8 percent interest annually, with inflation averaging 4 percent. After 20 years, your investment would have grown to over 450,000 naira. But your actual buying power would be less than 209,000 naira due to inflation. In simple terms, this means that 450,000 naira could only buy what 209,000 naira used to buy.

In Nigeria, only shares have been able to beat inflation for over a decade now. Other investment vehicles that have held the best against inflation include real estate and businesses. I call these three vehicles—shares, real estate, and businesses—the trinity of wealth because I believe they are wealth creators anywhere in the world. Your investment growth and rate of return must exceed inflation, or it will not make you financially independent.

The Principle of Compound Interest

Compound interest has been termed the eighth wonder of the world. It is a powerful financial and investment phenomenon that makes time work in our favor. Compound interest is what happens when investment earnings (a return on investment) are added to the principal (the original capital invested), forming a larger base on which earnings may accumulate. In other words, you receive interest on your interest, and as your investment base gets larger, it has the potential to grow faster. We touched on this concept earlier when we discussed the importance of time.

Let's look at another example. If you were to invest 1,000 dollars at an annual interest rate of 10 percent, at the end of the first year you would have earned 100 dollars in interest. Then if you were to reinvest this interest together with the initial investment, at the end of the second year you would have earned interest on 1,100 dollars. If the interest rate was still 10 percent, this means you would have earned 110 dollars in interest for the second year, and your balance would now be 1,210 dollars. The longer you invest, the greater the impact of compound interest.

The Principle of the Power of Annuity

An annuity is "a series of equal payments made over a fixed interval for a specific period." The principle of the power of annuity encompasses the concept that it is better to invest steadily over a period of time and allow consistent investing, time, and compound interest to work together to create wealth.

To see how these principles work together, let's consider another example. Imagine if you were to invest 18,000 naira *once*, at an annual interest rate of 20 percent. If you never added to your initial investment—except for reinvesting all the interest—at the end of 20 years, you would have an investment of over 690,000 naira.

Now imagine if you were to invest 18,000 naira *each year*, at an annual interest rate of 20 percent. If you added 18,000 each year to your initial investment, plus reinvested all interest earned, at the end of 20 years you would have an investment of over 3.3 million naira! Can you see the difference? It is better to invest consistently than only once. An investment of 18,000 naira per year equals 1,500 naira per month or 50 naira per day. This is affordable to most people, but how many will practice investing consistently? You can achieve financial independence and become rich and wealthy if you put these principles to work. I encourage you to start now!

The Universal Nature of These Principles

As I mentioned earlier, these principles can work anywhere in the world. All you need is to search out opportunities in your location. The concept of compound interest is one of the greatest financial miracles of our time. To some it appears almost magical and unbelievable, especially to those who lack financial intelligence.

To illustrate the universal nature of these principles, I would like to offer an example using American dollars. With an investment of five dollars per day (that is, 150 dollars per month or 1,800 dollars per year), anyone can start to create wealth, provided they find an investment vehicle that pays 10 percent annual interest. As you can see in the following chart, an investment of only five dollars per day, which earns annual interest that is reinvested and allowed to compound, will quickly grow.

At an interest rate of 10 percent, the investment will grow to over 29,000 dollars in ten years; at 12.5 percent the total will be over 33,000 dollars; at 15 percent the total will be over 37,000 dollars. A difference in interest of 5 percent results in a difference of over 8,000 dollars in ten years. This is why the vehicle you choose matters.

Investment of $150 Per Month or $1800 Per Year

YEARS	10%	12.5%	15%
1	1,980	2,050	2,070
2	3,928	4,078	4,180
3	6,176	6,384	6,607
4	8,593	8,985	9,398
5	11,252	11,908	12,607
6	14,177	15,196	16,298
7	17,395	18,895	20,542
8	20,934	23,056	25,423
9	24,827	27,738	31,036
10	29,110	33,005	37,491

Studies have shown that 100 dollars invested per month at an annual interest rate of 10 percent will grow to over 1 million dollars in 44 years. If you earn 25,000 dollars per year and save just 10 percent of your income in obedience to the 30:70 principal, you would be investing 2,500 dollars per year. At an annual interest rate of 10 percent, this would grow to nearly 1.8 million dollars in 44 years. If you consistently save and invest during the course of your working years, you will be well along the pathway to wealth.

I hope you are enjoying the journey on this pathway to wealth. From the financial intelligence bus stop, we moved on to the financial planning bus stop. Now it is time to consider the third and final bus stop on this pathway.

Chapter 9

The Pathway to Wealth— Financial Discipline

A thousand good intentions are not as powerful as a single action. Until you give attention to your intentions, your world will stand at attention and the world will not give you attention.

Financial discipline is the third and final bus stop on the pathway to wealth. It is at this bus stop that we separate the men from the boys; this is the boundary of separation. Many people have gained financial intelligence and established a financial plan, but they have never been disciplined enough to start executing their plan—adding action to their decision. Some have even begun to act but then have lacked the discipline to stick to their plan and stay consistent until their goal is achieved.

Everything we have learned, every principle we have discovered, is useless and powerless until it is applied and practiced. It is up to us to act, because nothing happens by chance. Principles will not work themselves; we must apply them. Our life and financial situation will remain the same until we make a decision to act on the information and principles we have learned.

Financial discipline is the final bus stop; it is the determining factor. Will you be disciplined enough to take action and stick to your plan for years? You can obtain all the financial intelligence you want and make all the plans you can, but unless you discipline yourself to follow through with the plan, you cannot achieve financial independence and become wealthy. It takes financial discipline to make it.

Distractions will come. Challenges will come. Temptations will come. Pressures will come. Unexpected expenses will come. Setbacks will come. Through it all, only those who have the discipline to stick to their plan eventually make it.

Just as a letter only arrives at its destination when a stamp sticks to it until the end, so you also will only arrive at your desired financial destination if you have the discipline to stick to your financial plan. Sticking to your plan means:

- you must stick to your budget;

- you must delay gratification;

- you must deny yourself some things;

- you must live on 70 percent of your income;

- you must avoid distraction;

- you must avoid emotional and impulse purchases;

- you must deny meeting the expectations of some people. In other words, you must avoid pleasing people to the detriment of your future;

- you must avoid living above your means, even if it seems like everyone else is doing it.

The ball is now in your court. The first part of this book has helped you to gain financial intelligence; it has provided information about establishing a financial plan, but it is your responsibility to now apply financial discipline so that you can arrive at a position of wealth. To help you apply financial discipline, I have two truths to share with you.

PARKINSON'S LAW

There is a well-known adage first articulated by Cyril Northcote Parkinson and referred to as Parkinson's Law. Simply stated it says, "Work expands so as to fill the time available for its completion." This law has sometimes been generalized as, "The demand upon a resource tends to expand to match the supply of the resource."

Paraphrasing this law and applying it to our subject, we can say that a man's expenses will always rise to meet his income and make him stay the same. This means that no matter how much additional income comes into a man's life, he will always increase his expenses to match the income. This makes it difficult for anyone to increase his net worth.

While Parkinson first included his law as part of a humorous essay, there is truth in it, and it has affected millions all over the world. Becoming a victim of this law has kept many people out of a place of wealth. Let's consider an example.

If a man earns 5,000 dollars per month, there are some things he stays away from because he cannot conveniently afford them, even though he is living comfortably without them. But if his salary increases to 8,000 dollars per month, instead of living the way he has been living and setting aside the additional income of 3,000 dollars each month as money to be invested, he increases his status in life by changing his diet, wardrobe, furniture, electronics, car, home, and so on. At the end of the day, even though his income has increased, nothing has really changed regarding his investments.

Are you a victim of Parkinson's Law? If so, break free today and change your story.

HOW TO MAKE MORE MONEY

The final truth I want to share with you to help you gain financial discipline is to emphasize that there are only two ways to make more money: either obtain additional income or reduce current expenditures.

You may think like many others, "If only I could get more money, then I would have money to invest," but you already have money to invest; you just do not want to accept this. Reducing current expenditures will make more money available even without any additional income. I am 100 percent certain that if you were to look at your life today, in light of all the information shared in this book, you would discover several areas where you could reduce or cut expenses. You can reduce expenses by eliminating some liabilities, delaying gratification in some areas, and avoiding spending money on things you can do without.

I have tried to help by making things as plain as possible. With all that you now know, there really is no excuse to fail or stay poor. Five years from today, everyone reading this book should be well along the pathway to wealth. All you need to do is apply all that you have already learned, together with all that you are about to learn in the remaining chapters. This requires discipline, but the reward is worth it.

I'd like to close this chapter with a story.

THE POOR ALWAYS CRY

Linus opened the trunk for the supermarket attendant to unload the bags into the car. It took quite some time for her to arrange them neatly so there would be enough space for everything. As the young female attendant turned to go, Richie pressed some crisp fifty-naira bills into her hand. She did not count because that would be impolite, but she estimated that there were about five bills. She nodded her head, glowing with excitement as she said, "Thank you." Linus gently closed the door after his boss had taken his seat. As he turned on the ignition, there was a fairly faint noise coming from somewhere and gradually getting louder.

"Richie! Richie!" Linus obviously paid no attention. Starting the car, he was ready to zoom off. "I can hear someone calling my name," Richie said without much certainty.

"Surely it's not for you; there are many Richies in Lagos," Linus responded somewhat nonchalantly.

"But the voice sounds familiar, like a voice I knew many years ago," Richie remarked.

Although much against his will, Linus turned off the engine and waited to convince his boss that no one was calling his name. A few feet away, Richie spotted Ben, one of his long-standing friends. They had been classmates at a university, and both had accepted jobs at Leventis Motors on the same day.

Richie spontaneously flung open his door, throwing himself at Ben. They had not seen each other for over six years, since Richie had resigned. From Richie's assessment, he could tell his friend was in bad shape.

"Richie! Just look at you. The god of fortune has really smiled on you." Ben was not given to hiding his feelings.

"My brother, it's the grace of God!" replied Richie.

"Hey, man, don't tell me that; you've got to show your brother the way, you know."

Richie smiled, somewhat embarrassed. He became a bit uncomfortable at Ben's insinuation that he was keeping some secret. "We need to talk," Richie eventually managed to say, breaking the cold silence that had begun to linger.

They agreed to meet at Richie's house the next day, Saturday. As Richie drove away in his metallic grey Lincoln Navigator, Ben stood watching, still wondering what in the world Richie had gotten into. He quickly assured himself that whatever it was, he wanted in.

The next day, as Ben trudged to Richie's house, he was still deep in thought and introspection. After being let through the gate of Richie's palatial mansion in Alvin Crescent, Ben was ushered into the house by a boy who obviously looked like Richie. Ben marveled at the overwhelming affluence lavishly exhibited in expensive high-tech equipment and artistic masterpieces.

Cool air flowed noiselessly from the air conditioner, making his ears cold even as he straightened the collar of his thick corduroy shirt. Ben watched with envy as Richie descended the stairs, which were covered in plush, beautiful carpet. Even the banister displayed opulence, with its meticulously carved detail.

Richie led Ben to an impressive sitting room, where they spoke at length. Much of the time was spent reminiscing about their mutual experience as undergrads at the University of Lagos and later as colleagues at Leventis. For Ben, it was a long and tortuous session. He could not wait to get to the heart of the matter.

Finally, Ben turned the conversation to what interested him most. "So, my friend, what exactly did you do that has set us apart in just a few years?"

Richie cleared his throat, took a deep breath, straightened his back, and leaned forward slightly. "Ben, let me start by telling you what I do not do," Richie began. "I never spend everything I get."

Richie's words caused Ben's phantom hope of a dramatic revelation to disappear. Ben's look of eager anticipation dissolved into one of melancholy. Still seeking answers, he garnered the courage to ask, "So what has that got to do with making money?"

"That, my friend, is the first step to becoming rich. Never spend all you get," Richie responded courteously but quite frankly.

"But I thought becoming rich was all about making and spending money," pressed Ben.

"No, Ben, you become rich by saving and investing money."

Ben turned his gaze from Richie and stared down at the floor. He remembered how even when they worked together Richie always saved money. Not a great amount, only about ten percent of his salary. But Richie saved with such consistency that others laughed at him and called him names. Unlike others, Richie wasn't into extravagant shopping. He spent his money buying only what was absolutely imperative or what could bring a return.

Somewhat cynically Ben inquired, "Richie, you aren't trying to tell me that your meager savings from when we worked together is what amassed this stupendous wealth. You aren't saying that, are you?"

By this point, Richie had realized how difficult it would be to help his friend break the backbone of poverty. He knew that if there was no transformation in attitude, there was no light at the end of the tunnel. Richie could not help Ben see the light, and Ben became disappointed. Ben stereotyped Richie as one of the typical rich men who were not happy to see others rise like them. Ben had hoped that his good friend would connect him to his business associates and help him with some start-up capital, but the conversation was not going as he had planned.

Ben had always been a politically minded person, and Richie wanted to know if his friend was still as passionate about politics as he used to be. "Are you still involved in politics?" asked Richie.

The question hit Ben like a stray bullet. But the answer jumped out spontaneously. "Richie, this country doesn't respect sound ideas. Only the rich get people to listen."

"Such a burning passion you had. Don't tell me you quit," Richie continued.

Ben sighed, a bit embarrassed. "It was the only thing to do. I had been told to shut up in meetings because I had no material proof of the suggestions I was raising."

Richie did not push the matter further. He knew that nobody listened to a poor man. As a Christian, he also remembered the words of King Solomon, that "the poor man's wisdom is despised, and his words are not heard." Richie felt that there was also no need to tell Ben that he was being offered a senatorial ticket by one of the leading political parties.

Ben wanted a quick fix for his poverty ailment. He wasn't open to the hypothesis being postulated by his friend. So he left hurting, a totally disappointed and dejected man.

While the two men were talking, Richie's ten-year-old son, Junior, was observing everything from a nearby room. As soon as the visitor was gone, he joined Richie and began asking questions. Richie was always ready to grant his son's impromptu interviews.

"Daddy, why does your friend look so broke?" Junior asked.

Richie thought for a moment. "Because he's broke."

"Why is he broke?"

"Because he's poor," responded Richie.

"Why is he poor?"

"Because he has the habit of the poor."

"What is the habit of the poor?"

"They pay everyone else except themselves," explained Richie. That day's encounter caused Richie to think, and he summed up the experience for his son with this expression, "It would be easier to sell winter jackets in the Sahara desert than for a poor mind to enter the kingdom of the wealthy."

Chapter 10

Spiritual Vehicles of Wealth Creation

*Spiritual investment is the foundation and security
for all physical investments, while physical
investment is the harvest channel and
completion of all spiritual investment.*

There are two categories of wealth creation vehicles: spiritual and physical. It is essential for anyone who desires to be truly rich and wealthy to have both types of vehicles in place. True wealth is comprised of seven components: faith in God, strategic relationships, material possessions, money, experiences in life, knowledge and skill, and health. To obtain these requires focusing on both the spiritual and physical.

Many live their whole lives only focusing on the physical while ignoring the spiritual. Others only focus on the spiritual while neglecting the physical. Such imbalance has caused shame and sorrow for many because one is not complete without the other. Spiritual investment is the foundation and security for all physical investments, while physical investment is the harvest channel and completion of all spiritual investment.

Christians are poor today for many reasons, but one reason is that while the Church has taught extensively on spiritual investment, little or nothing has been taught about physical investment. Due to this imbalance in the Church, many spend years giving and giving without becoming wealthy. They give and yet have no channel in place for their harvest to come.

If we give without using the power God gives to get wealth, it will amount to nothing. If we give without practicing investment principles, it too will amount to nothing. Such giving will only help to get some of the components of wealth like health, faith, relationships, experiences, knowledge, and skill, but it will not help to get money and material assets.

Many people have been faithful in tithing for years, but they have no investment in place and wonder why they are still not wealthy. Can you imagine how wealthy they would be if they had been as faithful to invest 10 percent as they have been to tithe 10 percent? Tithing 5,000 naira per month amounts to 600,000 naira in 10 years or 1.2 million naira in 20 years. Investing 5,000 naira per month, at an annual interest rate of 20 percent, would result in over 1.8 million naira in 10 years and over 13 million naira in 20 years!

While some people focus only on the spiritual, others know only about physical investment; they have millions in physical investment but zero in spiritual investment. Due to this imbalance, they too lack complete wealth; even though they may have money and material things, they lack good health, good relationships, faith in God, and so on.

To have millions in physical investment is useless if you have a sickness consuming your millions. What good is it to have millions and yet lack a good home with your marriage and children intact? Having millions but lacking faith or covenant relationship with your Creator is also useless. As it says in the Book of Mark, "For what will it profit a man if he gains the whole world, and loses his own soul?" (Mark 8:36).

We need balance to become all that we need to be. Balance is vital for stability and completion. The next chapter will focus on physical investment vehicles. For now, let's look at spiritual investment vehicles.

FIRSTFRUITS

There are many Scriptures that speak about the concept of firstfruits, which includes the firstborn. In Exodus chapter 13, we read, "Then the Lord spoke to Moses, saying, 'Consecrate to Me all the firstborn, whatever opens the womb among the children of Israel, both of man and beast; it is Mine'" (Exod. 13:1-2). Later in the same chapter, Moses says:

> And it shall be, when the Lord brings you into the land of the
> Canaanites, as He swore to you and your fathers, and gives it to
> you, that you shall set apart to the Lord all that open the womb,

that is, every firstborn that comes from an animal which you have; the males shall be the Lord's.... And all the firstborn of man among your sons you shall redeem. So it shall be, when your son asks you in time to come, saying, "What is this?" that you shall say to him, "By strength of hand the Lord brought us out of Egypt, out of the house of bondage. And it came to pass, when Pharaoh was stubborn about letting us go, that the Lord killed all the firstborn in the land of Egypt, both the firstborn of man and the firstborn of beast. Therefore I sacrifice to the Lord all males that open the womb, but all the firstborn of my sons I redeem." It shall be as a sign on your hand and as frontlets between your eyes, for by strength of hand the Lord brought us out of Egypt (Exodus 13:11-16).

Firstfruits is one of the spiritual vehicles. It refers to giving the first of everything to God as a sign that we acknowledge His ownership of all things. As I said before, whatever we do with the first affects the rest. As it says in Romans, "For if the firstfruit is holy, the lump is also holy; and if the root is holy, so are the branches" (Rom. 11:16). Leviticus clearly describes the concept of offering firstfruits:

And the Lord spoke to Moses, saying, "Speak to the children of Israel, and say to them:'When you come into the land which I give you, and reap its harvest, then you shall bring a sheaf of the firstfruits of your harvest to the priest. He shall wave the sheaf before the Lord, to be accepted on your behalf; on the day after the Sabbath the priest shall wave it. And you shall offer on that day, when you wave the sheaf, a male lamb of the first year, without blemish, as a burnt offering to the Lord'" (Leviticus 23:9-12).

What do we mean when we say *firstfruits* today? Firstfruits include: salary, harvest, income from any labor, and any increase. We can even acknowledge things like our first child, our first car, or our first house by making a special monetary offering to God in thanks.

Proverbs says, "Honor the Lord with your possessions, and with the firstfruits of all your increase; so your barns will be filled with plenty, and your vats will overflow with new wine" (Prov. 3:9-10). We need to have a revelation about firstfruits and act in faith in order to receive the full benefits.

TITHES

Tithes are another powerful spiritual investment vehicle. Tithing means to give 10 percent of all income to God faithfully and continually. In fact, it means giving back as the tithe already is the Lord's. We see this in Leviticus, where it says, "And all the tithe of the land, whether of the seed of the land or of the fruit of the tree, is the Lord's. It is holy to the Lord" (Lev. 27:30).

The Book of Malachi describes the consequences of not tithing and also the blessings of tithing. Here we read about people who are cursed because they did not follow God's laws, but we also read of the abundant blessing He promises if they do start tithing.

> *"For I am the Lord, I do not change; therefore you are not consumed, O sons of Jacob. Yet from the days of your fathers you have gone away from My ordinances and have not kept them. Return to Me, and I will return to you," says the Lord of hosts. "But you said, 'In what way shall we return?' Will a man rob God? Yet you have robbed Me! But you say, 'In what way have we robbed You?' In tithes and offerings. You are cursed with a curse, for you have robbed Me, even this whole nation. Bring all the tithes into the storehouse, that there may be food in My house, and try Me now in this," says the Lord of hosts, "If I will not open for you the windows of heaven and pour out for you such blessing that there will not be room enough to receive it. And I will rebuke the devourer for your sakes, so that he will not destroy the fruit of your ground, nor shall the vine fail to bear fruit for you in the field," says the Lord of hosts; "and all nations will call you blessed, for you will be a delightful land," says the Lord of hosts* (Malachi 3:6-12).

After reading about such curses and blessings, I wonder why anyone would not tithe. Tithing is a powerful principal that redeems the remaining 90 percent we have and unlocks great blessings upon us.

OFFERINGS

Offerings are another powerful investment vehicle. Offerings are that which we give above—or in addition to—the tithe. Genesis describes how the Lord responded to Noah's offerings. It says that the offering smelled like a soothing aroma to the Lord and that He said He would "never again curse the ground for man's sake" nor would He "again destroy every living thing" (see Gen. 8:21). Deuteronomy explains that each should give according to how he has been blessed:

"Three times a year all your males shall appear before the Lord your God in the place which He chooses: at the Feast of Unleavened Bread, at the Feast of Weeks, and at the Feast of Tabernacles; and they shall not appear before the Lord empty-handed. Every man shall give as he is able, according to the blessing of the Lord your God which He has given you" (Deuteronomy 16:16-17).

We should never come into God's presence (or any church service) empty-handed. The Bible describes the difference between one who gives and one who withholds. In Proverbs we read, "There is one who scatters, yet increases more; and there is one who withholds more than is right, but it leads to poverty" (Prov. 11:24). And in Second Corinthians, it says:

But this I say: He who sows sparingly will also reap sparingly, and he who sows bountifully will also reap bountifully. So let each one give as he purposes in his heart, not grudgingly or of necessity; for God loves a cheerful giver. And God is able to make all grace abound toward you, that you, always having all sufficiency in all things, may have an abundance for every good work. As it is written: "He has dispersed abroad, He has given to the poor; His righteousness endures forever." Now may He who supplies seed to the sower, and bread for food, supply and multiply the seed you have sown and increase the fruits of your righteousness (2 Corinthians 9:6-10).

The idea that by holding on tightly we may actually end up having less may seem to go against common sense, but that is the paradoxical nature of the Lord. Offerings are seed for a harvest of blessings.

- Firstfruits lay the foundation.

- Tithes open the heavens.

- Offerings activate the harvest.

PARENTAL HONOR

The Book of Romans says, "Render therefore to all their due: taxes to whom taxes are due; customs to whom customs; fear to whom fear; honor to whom honor" (Rom. 13:7). The Book of Ephesians is even more specific regarding how we should treat our parents. It says:

> *"Honor your father and mother," which is the first commandment with promise: "that it may be well with you and you may live long on the earth"* (Ephesians 6:2-3).

One spiritual investment vehicle, which is ignored by many, is parental honor. Honoring our parents by sowing into their lives is vital. It releases blessings and acts as a catalyst to the covenant of long life. Whether our parents are rich or not, we need to periodically and consistently sow into their lives as we are able. This should not turn into a legalistic matter, but we should honor our parents as part of our spiritual investment.

PROPHETIC HONOR

Many places in the Bible speak of honor and of how we should treat others. The Book of Matthew records Jesus instructing His disciples about receiving others:

> *"He who receives you receives Me, and he who receives Me receives Him who sent Me. He who receives a prophet in the name of a prophet shall receive a prophet's reward. And he who receives a righteous man in the name of a righteous man shall receive a righteous man's reward. And whoever gives one of these little ones only a cup of cold water in the name of a disciple, assuredly, I say to you, he shall by no means lose his reward"* (Matthew 10:40-42).

In Galatians, we read about sowing and reaping and how we should do good to all, especially to other Christians:

> *...for whatever a man sows, that he will also reap. For he who sows to his flesh will of the flesh reap corruption, but he who sows to the Spirit will of the Spirit reap everlasting life. And let us not grow weary while doing good, for in due season we shall reap if we do not lose heart. Therefore, as we have opportunity, let us do good*

to all, especially to those who are of the household of faith (Galatians 6:7-10).

First Timothy says, "Let the elders who rule well be counted worthy of double honor, especially those who labor in the word and doctrine. For the Scripture says...'The laborer is worthy of his wages'" (1 Tim. 5:17-18). And in Philippians, Paul writes of how he was cared for by others in the Church:

Nevertheless you have done well that you shared in my distress. Now you Philippians know also that in the beginning of the gospel, when I departed from Macedonia, no church shared with me concerning giving and receiving but you only. For even in Thessalonica you sent aid once and again for my necessities. Not that I seek the gift, but I seek the fruit that abounds to your account. Indeed I have all and abound. I am full, having received from Epaphroditus the things sent from you, a sweet-smelling aroma, an acceptable sacrifice, well pleasing to God. And my God shall supply all your need according to His riches in glory by Christ Jesus (Philippians 4:14-19).

Prophetic honor is another powerful investment vehicle that some people seldom observe; others who do, don't do it consistently. We should strongly consider sowing into any minister of God who blesses or affects our life positively. This is a vital spiritual investment vehicle that has undeniable results.

Welfare and Benevolence to the Poor and Needy

The Bible is quite clear about how we should treat the poor and needy. In Leviticus, the Lord spoke to Moses about this, saying:

And you shall not glean your vineyard, nor shall you gather every grape of your vineyard; you shall leave them for the poor and the stranger: I am the Lord your God...When you reap the harvest of your land, you shall not wholly reap the corners of your field when you reap, nor shall you gather any gleaning from your harvest. You shall leave them for the poor and for the stranger: I am the Lord your God (Leviticus 19:10; 23:22).

Deuteronomy also describes how we should be generous toward the poor:

> *"If there is among you a poor man of your brethren, within any of the gates in your land which the Lord your God is giving you, you shall not harden your heart nor shut your hand from your poor brother, but you shall open your hand wide to him and willingly lend him sufficient for his need, whatever he needs. Beware lest there be a wicked thought in your heart...and you give him nothing, and he cry out to the Lord against you, and it become sin among you. You shall surely give to him, and your heart should not be grieved when you give to him, because for this thing the Lord your God will bless you in all your works and in all to which you put your hand. For the poor will never cease from the land; therefore I command you, saying, 'You shall open your hand wide to your brother, to your poor and your needy, in your land'"* (Deuteronomy 15:7-11).

Proverbs describes the benefits of giving to the poor, and it also provides a warning about what will happen if we ignore the needy:

> *He who has pity on the poor lends to the Lord, and He will pay back what he has given....Whoever shuts his ears to the cry of the poor will also cry himself and not be heard* (Proverbs 19:17; 21:13).

The above Scriptures are self-explanatory. We should make provision for those less privileged as part of our spiritual investment. It is a vital spiritual investment vehicle that many people ignore. They invest in physical vehicles but never give to charitable causes that help the less privileged.

MISSIONS

All the Scriptures we examined, in regards to welfare and benevolence toward the poor and needy, also apply to missions. We should give some of our money and resources to assist missionaries and missions. This is another spiritual investment vehicle.

VOWS

Vows are also a spiritual investment vehicle. A vow moves God to intervene on our behalf. I consider vows secret weapons of supernatural intervention. In First Samuel, we read the story of Hannah, a woman full of sorrow because she had no children. She made a vow, and God heard and responded to her need:

And she was in bitterness of soul, and prayed to the Lord and wept in anguish. Then she made a vow and said, "O Lord of hosts, if You will indeed look on the affliction of Your maidservant and remember me, and not forget Your maidservant, but will give Your maidservant a male child, then I will give him to the Lord all the days of his life, and no razor shall come upon his head."…Then they arose early in the morning and worshiped before the Lord…and the Lord remembered her. So it came to pass in the process of time that Hannah conceived and bore a son, and called his name Samuel, saying, "Because I have asked for him from the Lord" (1 Samuel 1:10-11;19-20).

The Book of Psalms provides great encouragement regarding vows. It says, "Offer to God thanksgiving, and pay your vows to the Most High. Call upon Me in the day of trouble; I will deliver you, and you shall glorify Me" (Ps. 50:14-15). And Ecclesiastes provides a sober warning about the importance of keeping any vow we make:

When you make a vow to God, do not delay to pay it; for He has no pleasure in fools. Pay what you have vowed—better not to vow than to vow and not pay. Do not let your mouth cause your flesh to sin, nor say before the messenger of God that it was an error. Why should God be angry at your excuse and destroy the work of your hands? For in the multitude of dreams and many words there is also vanity. But fear God (Ecclesiastes 5:4-7).

SEEDS OF FAITH

Seeds of faith are very powerful spiritual investment vehicles. Genesis describes how Noah offered such seeds to God:

Then Noah built an altar to the Lord, and took of every clean animal and of every clean bird, and offered burnt offerings on the altar. And the Lord smelled a soothing aroma. Then the Lord said in His heart, "I will never again curse the ground for man's sake, although the imagination of man's heart is evil from his youth; nor will I again destroy every living thing as I have done. While the earth remains, seedtime and harvest, cold and heat, winter and summer, and day and night shall not cease" (Genesis 8:20-22).

These are seeds we sow in faith to God toward the release of a particular harvest. For example, we can sow a seed of faith toward something in particular that we want God to do for us.

SACRIFICIAL SEEDS

Psalms describes sacrificial seeds, the final spiritual investment vehicle:

"Gather My saints together to Me, those who have made a covenant with Me by sacrifice...."Those who sow in tears shall reap in joy. He who continually goes forth weeping, bearing seed for sowing, shall doubtless come again with rejoicing, bringing his sheaves with him (Psalm 50:5; 126:5-6).

Sacrificial seed is a master key for stupendous wealth creation. Many give, but only a few make sacrifices and give sacrificially. Some give sacrificially once in a while, but very few do it consistently. Living a life of sacrificial giving keeps Heaven perpetually open.

Each of these ten spiritual investment vehicles we have examined have their place, importance, and benefits. A wise person will make sure that none of them is ignored. I encourage you to be sure your life consists of the ten vehicles in balanced proportion so that you may get the full and complete benefit of spiritual investment.

Chapter 11

Physical Vehicles of Wealth Creation

*If you are not born with a silver spoon in your
mouth, create a silver spoon with your mind
(an investment mentality) because nobody
really came into this world with money.*

As I mentioned in the previous chapter, the Church has extensively taught about spiritual vehicles without balancing this teaching with lessons about physical investment vehicles. Operating in spiritual vehicles is very important. Remember, they are the foundation and security for all physical investments. However, in order to enjoy complete prosperity and wealth, we must take time to learn of the physical vehicles. This is what we will consider in this chapter.

PAID EMPLOYMENT

Paid employment is a physical vehicle that gives us access to money we can invest in other vehicles. Without an income source, we may not have money to invest. Paid employment together with an investment mentality is a powerful vehicle because it helps us move from earned income to portfolio or passive income.

Paid employment may also help us rise to become senior executives with a good paycheck, stock options, bonuses, profit sharing, and so on. As we reach this level, we should have more money to invest because then we will most likely have an official car, official house, or other benefits. This means we should now use our money to invest heavily.

But no matter how highly placed we are in paid employment or how big our paycheck gets, without an investment mentality we can still end up in shame. Stories abound of people who rose to high positions and great salaries, but they lived a wasted life of unrestrained and unwise spending, accumulating liabilities. When they lost their jobs, they lost everything. When the job ceased, so did the official car, house, bonuses, and so on.

Do not allow paid employment to be your only vehicle, or you may end up in shame and poverty.

INHERITANCE OR WEALTH TRANSFER

Another vehicle that is available to only a few people on earth is the inheritance vehicle. Less than 10 percent of those who are extremely rich and wealthy, in any economy, inherited their wealth. And the number continues to drop. Over 90 percent of children of successful people usually end up failing, since they live by the wealth from someone else's labor, which cost them nothing to inherit. Due to an inability to manage this inherited wealth, they lavish it on liabilities and end up having nothing to transfer to their own children.

Before wealth is transferred by inheritance, wisdom demands that the beneficiary should be mentored and taught how to develop an investment mentality. Beneficiaries should be made to acquire financial intelligence, management competence, entrepreneurial skills, and hands-on training so as to ensure that the wealth does not disappear in their lifetime. If this is not done, inheritors of wealth often end up like lottery winners—over 90 percent of them become poor in less than two years.

MONEY MARKETS

Money markets refer to financial instruments put in place for short-term transactions. They are offered by banks, finance houses, discount houses, and other financial institutions outside the capital market. They include, but are not limited to: savings or checking accounts, fixed or call deposits, and treasury bills.

As I mentioned earlier, everyone should have a savings account. This will enable you to save money, earn interest, and increase your money. Though the interest rate for savings accounts is usually small and cannot beat inflation, having one is still a vital step that must be taken to develop discipline and a saving mind-set. It is the lowest level of investment recommended.

Even Jesus taught about earning interest. The Book of Matthew contains the parable of the talents. In this story, three men are given money, and each invests it differently. Two turn a profit, but one hides his master's money in the ground because he is fearful of losing that which he was given. When the master returns, he scolds this man saying, "So you ought to have deposited my money with the bankers, and at my coming I would have received back my own with interest" (Matt. 25:27).

Checking accounts do not usually earn interest. Often they involve fees, but they also provide a way to distribute and receive payments. This type of account facilitates transactions. If you want to trade in stocks, it will also be helpful to have such an account because you can deposit dividends into a checking account. Apart from the fact that it usually pays no interest, a checking account does have its uses and benefits.

Fixed deposits are time-based accounts where you leave money for 30, 60, 90, or 180 days and receive a fixed interest rate on the amount you deposited. These usually pay higher interest than savings accounts, and the interest rate is negotiable. This means you can discuss the rate you want to receive based on the size of the deposit and how long you are willing to leave it in the bank.

Call deposits are similar to fixed deposits, but they have different rules. With fixed deposits, you cannot collect your money until the agreed time has passed. If you choose to withdraw money early, you will lose either part or all of the interest. But call deposits are usually for a shorter period of time, and all you need to do to get your money early is to notify the bank before you withdraw it (usually 24 hours' notice). Though you may get lower interest rates with a call deposit than with a fixed deposit, they both still pay a higher rate than savings accounts.

Treasury bills are certificates that the central bank of a country makes available on behalf of the government. Governments use these to borrow money from the public, and in exchange they pay fixed interest to those who buy and hold these certificates for a period of time.

CAPITAL MARKETS

Capital markets refer to investment vehicles that work long-term. They are instruments used to raise capital for companies and organizations. This is a place for investors to grow their idle funds. They include, but are not limited to: stocks or shares, mutual funds, and government bonds.

Stocks or Shares

A stock or share is a unit of capital for a company. If you invest in a company by buying a particular amount of shares in that company, it means that in essence you own part of that company. What percentage of the company you own is directly related to the total number of stocks or shares available for that company. The value of your investment can increase or decrease depending on whether the price of stocks or shares rises or falls. For example, if you buy 100,000 dollars worth of shares in a company but then the price of shares drops, the value of your initial investment also decreases. There are three ways to make money with stocks or shares. Let's briefly look at each.

Price or capital appreciation describes what happens if the price of shares increases. For example if you buy ten dollars worth of shares, and the price of shares later doubles, you will have made 100 percent profit. Your shares would now be worth twenty dollars. At this point, you could sell all your shares and walk away, or you could choose to sell only half of them. This means that you are cashing out (regaining) your initial investment, and the remaining shares are free and clear (profit). Or you could choose to leave everything invested. It all depends on your financial plan and goal.

Bonus shares are used by many companies at the end of a profitable year as a way to reward shareholders. They declare bonuses and gives additional shares to investors. They could give one bonus share for every share owned, or one for every four, and so on. This helps to increase the size of your portfolio.

Dividends are another way that companies reward investors. At the end of a fiscal year, companies set aside a portion of their profit, which is approved by the board of directors but subject to acceptance by the annual general meeting of such an organization. These dividends are paid to investors, and they may not look like much, but for larger investors dividend payments can run into the millions.

When you add up these three ways to increase your wealth, I believe you will discover that investing in stocks is worth the risk, time, and resources. This is because in the end, stocks provide the possibility to make money without working for it, and this is a substantial benefit. Your money is working to make more money for you.

Mutual Funds

Mutual funds or unit trusts are funds created by investment houses like stock broker firms or finance houses. They pool investors' funds together and invest them on their behalf in different investment channels like oil and gas, manufacturing, real estate, and so on. Mutual funds vary from firm to firm. They tend to be considered less risky than direct investment in the stock market because the investment is diversified. In other words, one mutual fund is usually invested in several different companies over several different industries.

The fund manager or fund administrator—the company in charge of these funds—bears responsibility for choosing which companies to invest in. This is not the case with direct investment in the stock market, where it is the investor or shareholder who chooses which company or companies to invest in. Mutual funds are another way to grow your money while leaving the day-to-day decisions in the hands of a fund manager.

Government Bonds

A government bond is a certificate promising repayment of debt. This is like the government borrowing money from you through the bond and promising to pay back your initial investment, plus interest at a fixed rate, on a specific date. Companies can also issue bonds called debentures.

Whether or not you fully understand all these types of capital market investments, I encourage you to start from any point and begin to create your own wealth. The earlier you begin, the better.

REAL ESTATE

Real estate is real investment. It is a very powerful vehicle of wealth creation and wealth preservation. Every truly wealthy person has investments in real estate. Investing in property not only provides potential for rental income, but property usually always appreciates in value.

There are many benefits to owning real estate. You can live in it and free yourself from rent for life. If you are renting it out to someone else, you can increase the rent even though the land and house size remain the same. You can sell the property later with great profit.

I believe everyone should endeavor to own his or her own property because no one should live and die a tenant. As a tenant, you indirectly finance the landlord's expenses and liabilities. As a tenant, your landlord is, in a way, a lord over you. As a tenant, any money you spend on the property does not increase your wealth, but it helps your landlord increase the value of his property.

As you work and make money, your money should be invested. Later your investment can be converted into portfolio assets like stocks and passive assets like real estate. Investing in properties has many advantages. For example, with real estate you can actually see what your money has purchased. Also, property values and rent normally rise above inflation. Finally, property can become collateral for a loan.

There are, however, some challenges related to real estate investment. You must have sizeable capital to buy or build. Even if you plan to carry a mortgage, you still usually need to have enough for a down payment. Also, real estate is not a liquid asset. It takes time to sell properties, which can be a problem if you need cash fast. Finally, property management can be a challenging job unless you hand it over to competent agents.

There are several vital facts about real estate: First, land may not increase in size, but it will continue to increase in value. Second, location matters in real estate investment. Finally, the population and development around your real estate matters.

I have heard it said that the future is cheap if you buy it today. You may not have money to buy expensive land in a prime location today, but you can position yourself for the future of development.

Cities always develop toward the outskirts. So, real estate at the outskirts of a city may be cheaper now, but in time it should increase in value.

Types of Real Estate Investment

There are several types of real estate investment. Let's briefly consider some of them. You can buy land in undeveloped areas, wait for few years, and sell when development reaches your area and value has increased. You can buy land, build a house or houses, and sell the houses or rent them out. You can buy a house, keep it for a while, and then resell. Or you can buy a house and rent it out.

You can also purchase by means of a presale. This means that you buy a house, a shop, or some property *before* it is actually built or developed, and then you can sell it once it is completed. When you buy like this, usually you only pay a deposit to secure the purchase and select a location. By the time development is completed, you can sell your property and walk away with a profit, or you can turn it into a rental property.

Another way to invest is to buy dilapidated or abandoned properties, develop and bring them to life, and then sell them or rent them out. You can also look for homes that are in foreclosure and are being sold at auction. Such houses are usually available at far below the market value. Later you can sell them or turn them into rental properties.

Estate development is yet another type of real estate investment. This involves buying a large piece of land, developing it into an estate, selling plots to others who join in the development. Alternatively, you can take care of installing all the utilities and then sell the plots as serviced plots with utilities, or you can even build all the houses and then sell or rent them.

As you can see, the possibilities in real estates are numerous, and with financial intelligence and the right information, you can build wealth through real estate.

BUSINESS

Owning your own business is considered one of the most powerful vehicles of wealth creation, if not the most powerful. In a previous chapter, I described shares, real estate, and business as the trinity of wealth creation. I venture to say that any truly wealthy man or woman has investments in one or more of these three areas. There is no wealth or financial independence without one, two, or all three of these.

There are several benefits to owning a business. It is the fastest route and vehicle to wealth. It has limitless possibilities and potential to generate profit in the shortest time. If your business is successful, you can make in one deal or one month what others make in a year. By owning a business you have freedom and control of everything. And it is a powerful vehicle for staying above inflation.

First Thessalonians says that we should "aspire to lead a quiet life, to mind your own business, and to work with your own hands...that you may lack nothing" (see 1 Thess. 4:11-12). In the Contemporary English Version it says we are to "work hard" (see 1 Thess. 4:11 CEV). These and other Scriptures clearly tell us that part of God's plan is for us to work and not be lazy.

As we have seen over and over again, part of financial intelligence is developing entrepreneurial skills and management capabilities. Business owners will only succeed when they have an entrepreneurial spirit and skills in place, along with business management abilities. As you work, make sure you spend time learning about structures, management, and developing skills that will help you when you finally start your own business. Some people plan to start their own business when they retire, but they fail to use their working years to gather the skills and abilities required to succeed.

Why You Should Move From Employee to Employer

In an earlier chapter, we looked at the life of Jacob as an example of one who had an investment mentality. We can also see in the story of Jacob why it is not always good to be the employee. In Genesis, we read how he was mistreated by his employer:

> So Jacob sent and called Rachel and Leah to the field, to his flock, and said to them, "I see your father's countenance, that it is not favorable toward me as before; but the God of my father has been with me. And you know that with all my might I have served your father. Yet your father has deceived me and changed

my wages ten times, but God did not allow him to hurt me"
(Genesis 31:4-7).

It is not an employer's job to make us rich; it is our responsibility. In order to be rich, we should have a plan to move from being an employee to being an employer.

There are several negative aspects to being an employee, as I already mentioned in an earlier chapter. Being an employee hinders our financial and material progress because someone else determines our salary and our advancement. Being an employee lacks security; it leaves us at the mercy of our employer's favor. As an employee, our wages are usually set at what our employer thinks they should be, which is often below our real worth and value.

Often employers do not value their workers until a worker says he wants to leave. We see this in the story of Jacob. After Rachel gave birth, Jacob told Laban (her father and his employer) that he wanted to leave (see Gen. 30:25-26). Laban pleaded with Jacob to stay saying, "Name me your wages, and I will give it" (see Gen. 30:28). Why did Laban not allow Jacob to name his wage earlier? I believe it was because Laban did not truly value Jacob, but now he recognized his worth and feared losing such a good employee.

Being an employee can keep us under constant fear—fear of losing our job of offending our boss, and of losing our salary. As an employee, we give our most valuable years in exchange for a salary. Our time, talent, virtue, knowledge, skills, energy, and influence are used to create more wealth for our employer, and we may or may not reap the benefits of our labor.

As an employee, our personal visions and dreams are subordinate to the corporate vision and mission. Being an employee that means someone else determines when we wake up, when we get home, where and how we live. As an employee, we may even be viewed with suspicion—especially regarding acquisitions. Again, we see this with Jacob:

> *Now Jacob heard the words of Laban's sons, saying, "Jacob has taken away all that was our father's, and from what was our father's he has acquired all this wealth." And Jacob saw the countenance of Laban, and indeed it was not favorable toward him as before* (Genesis 31:1-2).

Upon retirement, after decades of faithful service, what awaits employees? In the past, employees may have received a suitable pension, but in today's ever-changing economy they are more likely to receive a limited retirement benefit, if anything at all. Often this is only enough to cover a small part of living expenses.

I encourage you to begin to strategize how to run your own business and provide for your own house now and forever.

A Word of Balance

I believe it is important to give a word of balance here so that what I have shared regarding employment is not misunderstood. Almost everyone will start out as an employee, and this is a vehicle all its own. Our faithfulness at this level—both to our boss and the establishment—determines whether we will ever get our own business started and be successful. As it says in the Book of Luke:

> *He who is faithful in what is least is faithful also in much; and he who is unjust in what is least is unjust also in much. Therefore if you have not been faithful in the unrighteous mammon, who will commit to your trust the true riches? And if you have not been faithful in what is another man's, who will give you what is your own?* (Luke 16:10-12)

Our time as an employee is not a waste. We should use it to gather experience and skills that will prepare us to succeed on our own. Your employer is not your enemy; do not sow what you do not want to reap in the future. Remember, when you start your own business you will also have staff, and what you sow is what you will reap.

There are many things we should strive to learn while working for others. These are skills that will help us in our own business. We should learn how to sell ourselves and how to sell products and services. It is important to learn communications skills—both written and verbal. It is essential to earn how to manage. This includes managing people, projects, money, and time. It is also critical that we learn to manage ourselves, our life, and our home.

Questions to Answer Before Going Into Business

There are many questions to answer before starting a business. Below is a list to help you evaluate where you stand. Please take the time to carefully consider each one.

- How organized are you?
- Do you have a competitive spirit?
- Are you a risk-taker or risk-dodger?
- What experience or skills have you gained that will help you in business?
- Are you in good health?
- Can you lead and manage people?
- Do you have a high energy level, or do you get tired easily after 2 or 3 hours?
- Are you self-confident; can you press on when things go wrong?
- Are you ready to make short-term sacrifices for long-term benefits?
- Can you delay gratification and postpone pleasure?
- Is your spouse supportive of your business dream?
- Can you make others see the benefit of what you do?
- Do you have a natural flair for business?
- Do you enjoy mixing with people?
- Have you conceived or developed a winning business idea, product, or service?
- Are you enthusiastic about your dream?
- Do you have the resources (spiritual, material, physical, financial, human) that you need?
- Do you have an investment mentality?
- Do you have financial intelligence?
- Do you have a plan and a goal in place?

How to Start a Business of Your Own

After evaluating yourself using the above questions, you should have a better idea of your strengths and weaknesses. Now it is time to consider what you are good at. It may not necessarily be what you studied in school. Consider these questions:

- What you are trained to do?

- In what ways are you gifted or talented?

- What you are anointed or inspired to do?

To start a business, you need to have a clear picture of what you really want to achieve. It is wise to submit yourself to a process of mentoring to gain experience. Next, carry out a feasibility study to identify challenges and competition in advance, and consider solutions to potential challenges.

One key is to learn from your past and from others by reading biographies, success stories, and bankruptcy stories. It is important to continually update, upgrade, and inspire yourself. Be patient, be persistent, and *never give up.* Keep your dream alive, stick to the rules, and give God His rightful place. Follow these tips and you will make it.

How to Generate Business Ideas

Some people have the desire to start a business, but they are not sure of exactly what they want to do. There are many ways to generate business ideas. For example, you can take an existing product, add value or new benefits to it, and offer it at the existing price, or perhaps even less. Or you can take an ordinary product, strip it down to its basics, and offer the substance of it at a reduced price. You can add or remove packaging from a product or service. You can package a convenience item—"something made easy."

Consider how to add speed of delivery to a basic product or service. Use design or packaging to enhance a basic appliance or product. Use design to relieve stress from life. Generalize a hoarded technology or idea. Offer better value by combining attributes.

Look for a need and fill it. Solve problems for people. Bring out inspirational products. These are just some of the ways to generate ideas; I am sure you can think of more on your own.

How to Raise Capital for Your Business Idea

Many people have business ideas but lack the capital required or the wisdom to raise the capital. Regardless of the amount of the capital needed, these strategies can work anywhere in the world.

Consider using your personal savings, which you have built up by following the 30:70 principle. Think about approaching your family and friends. There might be mentors or angel investors who believe in and support your dream.

Perhaps you can sell some liabilities or assets. There may be cooperatives or thrift societies that can help. You may want to go into partnership or research how to obtain government grants or funding from non-profit organizations (NGOs). You may want to approach a bank for a loan.

Are there any gratuities or seasonal benefits (bonuses) that you could pour into your new business? Do you have something you could trade or barter? Perhaps you received an insurance settlement that could be used as seed money for your business.

You can always start with the idea from where you are; start small and see how it grows. Consider using the Internet for business or marketing purposes. Another option is to buy an existing business, with little or no money down. Finally, you may want to consider selling your idea and using the money from that sale to start a new business.

We have looked at the physical investment vehicles of paid employment, inheritance, money markets, capital markets, real estate, and business in great detail. It is now time to look briefly at a few remaining vehicles. We will not examine these as closely because they all fall under the category of business.

INTELLECTUAL PROPERTY

Intellectual property is a vehicle of wealth creation that has produced tremendous wealth for many. This includes inventions and anything else that pays royalties. Musicians, authors, actors, football players and other athletes all fall into this category. They have developed their skills and talents to a level where they generate wealth. They can write a book, sing a song, or introduce products or inventions that become a gold mine. Look into yourself; think about what you could create or produce that could become your own label or brand. When you produce something that becomes your inspiration, money can flow from it continually.

NETWORK OR MULTILEVEL MARKETING

Multilevel marketing—and marketing, in general—can become a vehicle of wealth creation. Choosing the right multilevel marketing, starting at the right time, and getting accurate information will determine the success of this vehicle. GNLD, Forever Living Product, and Tianshi, are all multilevel marketing products that many have testified to as being their own vehicle of wealth creation. Be sure to research before getting involved in such vehicles. Assess whether you have the time, energy, and all it takes to succeed. Remember: *investigate before you invest.*

INTERNET BUSINESSES

The emergence of the Internet changed many things around the world. Today, many have become wealthy through Internet businesses. Many home businesses have started and succeeded by doing business over the Internet. There are numerous books and materials that can educate you further on the "what and how" of Internet businesses. If this appeals to you, I encourage you get them.

INFORMATION BUSINESS

Information products are another vehicle of wealth. If you have information that people need, you can create wealth by packaging the information in books, tapes, CDs, videos, workbooks, curriculums, training, seminars, and courses. The same information can continue to bring you money in different formats and from different places. Organizations around the world have been built around selling information.

OTHER VEHICLES

There are many other vehicles that we will not examine, but this chapter should have provided you with numerous ideas. The most important thing is to make sure you have vehicles in place to take you from where you are, to where you desire to go. Do not forget—balance is vital. Both spiritual and physical vehicles are very important in order to have complete wealth.

Chapter 12

Multiple Streams of Income

The sea never runs dry because it receives
water from various rivers and streams.

There are no rich and wealthy individuals on earth today who have only one source of income. Even if their business is their only source, the business itself makes money from multiple sources. It is therefore very important for everyone who desires to become rich and wealthy to ensure that they have multiple sources of income. The secret of unimaginable oceanic wealth is multiple streams of income.

The sea or ocean never runs dry, whether in rainy or dry seasons. The sea stays alive and full at all times and during all seasons. When a dry season comes, ponds dry up, and lakes dry up, some rivers dry up, but nowhere in the world does the sea or ocean dry up. This is true because multiple bodies of water—lakes, ponds, streams, rivers—eventually find their way into the sea or ocean. The ocean receives from multiple streams, and even though all the streams do not flow with the same velocity or affect the ocean in the same way, they all have a part to play in the continual existence of the ocean.

To become like an ocean and stay wealthy no matter what comes your way, you need to establish different sources of income in your life. Then when some streams dry up during the dry season, others will still keep on flowing.

DIMENSIONS OF STREAMS

There are different dimensions of streams that exist in wealth creation. Let's look at some of them.

One-time streams are wealth streams where you work once and get paid once. In order to get paid again, you have to work again. This includes work such as sales, contracts, salaried employment, and so on.

Once-and-always streams are wealth streams where you work hard once, but you get paid continually for the initial labor. You do not have to work hard again to keep getting money from this stream. Operating a transportation business, owning rental properties, writing books, and releasing albums all fall under this category. For example, you only build a house once, but it keeps bringing in money. You only produce an album once, but it keeps earning money. You only write a book once, but it keeps generating money.

Free-flow streams are wealth streams where you do not even have to do anything. Instead, you put your money to work for you. The money does all the work while you enjoy the benefits. Stocks, bonds, mutual funds, and so on are included here.

As I mentioned earlier, there are three different types of income: earned, passive, and portfolio income. The three dimensions of streams correlate with these three categories:

DIMENSIONS OF STREAMS	TYPES OF INCOME
ONE-TIME STREAMS	EARNED INCOME
ONCE-AND-ALWAYS STREAMS	PASSIVE INCOME
FREE-FLOW STREAMS	PORTFOLIO INCOME

We all start out in the category of earned income or one-time streams, but we should work to convert our earned income to portfolio or passive income. Our investments should consist of all the dimensions of streams.

THE CREATOR'S INTENTION

The Lord God planted a garden eastward in Eden, and there He put the man whom He had formed. And out of the ground the Lord God made every tree grow that is pleasant to the sight and good for food. The tree of life was also in the midst of the garden, and the tree of the knowledge of good and evil. Now a river went out of Eden to water the garden, and from there it parted and became four riverheads. The name of the first is Pishon; it is the one which skirts the whole land of Havilah, where there is gold. And the gold of that land is good. Bdellium and the onyx stone are there. The name of the second river is Gihon; it is the one which goes around the whole land of Cush. The name of the third river is Hiddekel: it is the one which goes toward the east of Assyria. The fourth river is the Euphrates. Then the Lord God took the man and put him in the garden of Eden to tend and keep it (Genesis 2:8-15).

The above verses reveal the Creator's mind regarding wealth creation. When Adam came into existence, God planted a garden. In other words, He established a business and put Adam in charge as the managing director or CEO. I believe this reveals that God's perfect plan for us is to have a business of our own. Going further, we can see that out of the Garden of Eden (Eden Corporation) a river or stream came forth, but it did not remain a stream. The stream parted into four riverheads or four streams so that Adam would end up with multiple streams of income. I dare to say that God's perfect plan is that everyone should have at least four streams of income.

The primary stream that came out of Eden was not mentioned by name, but its purpose was stated, "to water the garden" (see Gen. 2:10). It later parted into four named rivers:

- The Pishon river goes around Havilah, where there is gold, good gold. There is also bdellium and onyx stone (see Gen. 2:11-12).

- The Gihon river goes around the land of Cush (see Gen. 2:13).

- The Hiddekel river goes toward the east of Assyria (see Gen. 2:14).

- The Euphrates river is the largest of all the rivers (see Gen. 2:14).

This is not a theological book, but if you study the meaning of each of the names given to the rivers, you will not only discover that they relate to some of the investment vehicles we have examined in previous chapters but also that they relate to geography and all continents of the earth. I believe this means that God wants us to have global relevance in our wealth creation, breaking geographical boundaries. I also believe it illustrates that God wants us to have different vehicles of wealth creation in place. How to we begin to do this? Let's look at a few strategies for creating multiple streams of income.

DISCOVER YOUR PRIMARY OR DOMINANT STREAM

Everyone should find out what his or her own Garden of Eden is. We each need to discover the primary river that will water our garden. This means finding what will water our life and empower us with seed money for investment. Watering the ground causes the ground to yield the seed in it. Acquiring income helps us manifest an investment mentality.

What is your primary or dominant stream? Is it paid employment, a career, a business of your own? You need to find out and start with it. My primary or dominant stream is the call of God upon my life as a pastor. So primarily I am a pastor, and every other thing I do is secondary. As a pastor, I teach people through books, tapes, seminars, and so on. If you haven't already, I encourage you to discover your primary or dominant stream.

USE FINANCIAL INTELLIGENCE AND AN INVESTMENT MENTALITY TO DEVELOP OTHER STREAMS—DIVERSIFICATION

As we discover our dominant stream, begin to operate within it, and continue to apply the 30:70 principle, this enables us to use the 10 to 20 percent savings or investments we have to activate other vehicles of wealth, and other streams.

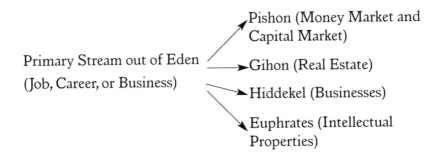

We start with one stream, which is our primary or dominant stream, but we should diversify and work toward having at least four of the physical vehicles of wealth creation we have examined earlier.

CONSOLIDATE EACH STREAM AND KEEP EXPANDING

Once we have been able to invest in other streams and have different vehicles of wealth producing income, we should ensure that we consolidate and establish each of the streams and vehicles fully. Then simply keep expanding until you become a force to be reckoned with on earth. This really is possible. Remember: the journey of a thousand miles begins with a single step. Do not think about what you do not have, but start with what you have from where you are. I'll see you at the top.

Chapter 13

Activating Generational Blessings

*Success without a successor equals
a successful failure.*

The concept of generational blessings is something that is understood and applied by some but not others. Many people—especially in the Church—lack an understanding of this concept, even though it is clearly a biblical concept.

Some people are more familiar with generational curses because that is what the Church dwells on more. Amazingly, some of the things that are labeled as generational curses are nothing but a product of generational ignorance. When ignorance is passed down from one generation to the next, the result of this ignorance is also passed down. After all, we teach our children only what we know. I believe that generational curses exist, and they are a biblical concept. However, we can change the story and begin to put generational blessings in place of generational curses.

Imbalance in the message of the Church has caused great problems for many believers. Apart from the generational curse issue, another issue that has caused problems in the Church is the prosperity message. The prosperity message tells believers that it is God's will to prosper them, but it neglects to explain the purpose for the prosperity. This has resulted in many materialistic, selfish, self-centered believers who now have prosperity without a posterity mentality.

Deuteronomy instructs us: "And you shall remember the Lord your God, for it is He who gives you power to get wealth, that He may establish His covenant which He swore to your fathers, as it is this day" (Deut. 8:18). The primary reason God prospers His people is to empower them to establish His Kingdom. World evangelism and missions cost money, and that is the primary reason for prosperity.

It is time to move from a prosperity mentality to a posterity mentality so that we can begin to activate generational blessings. After we prosper and have all the wealth in the world, what's next? *Posterity*, as we mentioned in an earlier chapter, is defined as "something that proceeds from you to others—to your descendents, to succeeding generations." A posterity mentality helps us to leave a legacy for the next generation. We need to develop a posterity mentality and become generational-minded in order to fulfill the purpose of God for our lives.

A posterity mentality and generational thinking are not natural to many people. This is because many of us have been trained and brought up to live for today or because our parents, leaders, and teachers did not know better. They could not teach us what they did not know, and they could not impact us with what they did not have. Everyone must make a conscious effort to personally develop a posterity mentality and generational thinking.

THE GENERATIONAL GOD

Our God is a generational God. When he had only Adam, he was speaking to Adam about his seed. When he spoke to Abraham, he spoke about his seed—even though it was a physical impossibility to have a child at the age of 75. God said to be fruitful because He saw children coming to fill the earth from generation to generation.

> *Then God blessed them, and God said to them, "Be fruitful and multiply; fill the earth and subdue it; have dominion over the fish of the sea, over the birds of the air, and over every living thing that moves on the earth"(Genesis 1:28).*

Later in Genesis, God spoke of generational warfare between the seeds of man and the devil, even when there had yet to be a single offspring. God said to the serpent, "And I will put enmity between you and the woman, and between your seed and her Seed; He shall bruise your head, and you shall bruise His heel" (Gen. 3:15).

Our God is a generational God. We see this in the story of Abraham. God spoke to Abraham about the families of the earth even when Abraham was yet to have a complete family of his own. God told Abraham, "In you all the families of the earth shall be blessed" (see Gen. 12:3). God was saying to Abraham, "I am a generational God. I have a generational plan. I possess generational blessings. I have more than enough to bless all the families of the earth from now until eternity."

God has enough to go around! God only needs people with generational thinking with whom He can work. God has made provision for every family on the earth to be taken care of, and that is why He blessed them all in Abraham.

Blessed means empowered, and it means power to get wealth. God has empowered each of us to become wealthy so that His Kingdom can be established, but not everyone will become wealthy unless they use the power. How can this dream of God come to pass if you and I do not become generational-minded and an extension of God on earth?

TENDING AND KEEPING

After getting the garden ready, God put man there "to tend and keep it" (see Gen. 2:15). Within these two purposes lie generational blessings.

To *tend* means to "cultivate, to compel to work, to make something produce." So God was telling Adam, "You must cultivate this garden; you must compel this garden to work; you must make this garden produce." This is God's purpose for all His children. God is saying, "I am a generational God with generational blessings. But in order for the blessing to flow from generation to generation, every one of you must have something to cultivate for increase, something to compel to work for you, something that produces for you."

To *keep* means to "protect, hedge about, and retain in ownership." So God is saying to Adam and to us all, "You must guide and protect what you are tending, so that it can continue to produce even after you die, and so that the next generation can benefit from it. Then it will be a generational blessing. You must retain ownership so that you can hand it over to the next generation."

Please note that practicing everything this book teaches will help to position you to activate generational blessings. This chapter is only aimed at helping to develop a posterity and generational mentality.

GENERATIONAL CURSES

God is posterity-minded both in terms of the positive and the negative. When He blesses, He expects it to become generational, and when He curses He also expects it to be generational—unless something is done about it. For example, we already read about how generational warfare began between man and the devil, and it still exists today (see Gen. 3:15).

In Genesis, we also read about the consequences Adam and Eve faced for disobeying God. God established pain in childbirth when He said to Eve, "I will greatly multiply your sorrow and your conception; in pain you shall bring forth children" (see Gen. 3:16). And to Adam, God described how work would now be more difficult:

> Then to Adam He said, "Because you have heeded the voice of your wife, and have eaten from the tree of which I commanded you, saying, 'You shall not eat of it': Cursed is the ground for your sake; in toil you shall eat of it all the days of your life. Both thorns and thistles it shall bring forth for you, and you shall eat the herb of the field. In the sweat of your face you shall eat bread till you return to the ground, for out of it you were taken; for dust you are, and to dust you shall return" (Genesis 3:17-19).

Such curses are generational until they are reversed by a covenant act. When God set in motion the curse on the earth, it was generational until something was done about it. Noah broke the curse with his seed and changed the story.

> Then Noah built an altar to the Lord, and took of every clean animal and of every clean bird, and offered burnt offerings on the altar. And the Lord smelled a soothing aroma. Then the Lord said in His heart, "I will never again curse the ground for man's sake, although the imagination of man's heart is evil from his youth; nor

will I again destroy every living thing as I have done. While the earth remains, seedtime and harvest, cold and heat, winter and summer, and day and night shall not cease" (Genesis 8:20-22).

The Book of Exodus clearly describes generational curses and blessings:

> *...I, the Lord your God, am a jealous God, visiting the iniquity of the fathers upon the children to the third and fourth generations of those who hate Me, but showing mercy to thousands, to those who love Me and keep My commandments* (Exodus 20:5-6).

Here we see that when God curses, it goes from generation to generation, but this is also true of God's blessings, even more so. Did you notice that though He said the iniquity would be punished to the third and fourth generation, He said mercy would continue for a thousand generations? Compare four to thousands. This shows the level of God's mercy, that God is more a God of generational blessings than a God of generational curses.

Why then are generational curses still present today? This is simply because man continues to extend them due to his continuous iniquity and idolatry.

Generational Blessings

When God spoke to Abraham, He established a generational blessing with him that extended to generations after him. God became the God of Abraham, Isaac, Jacob, Joseph, Benjamin, David, and you and me. In Genesis chapter 22, we read how God promised to bless Abraham and multiply his descendants:

> *Blessing I will bless you, and multiplying I will multiply your descendants as the stars of the heaven and as the sand which is on the seashore; and your descendants shall possess the gate of their enemies. In your seed all the nations of the earth shall be blessed, because you have obeyed My voice* (Genesis 22:17-18).

We can see this is a generational blessing because God refers "all the nations of the earth" being blessed through Abraham's seed (see Gen. 22:18). Genesis chapter 26 speaks of God blessing Abraham's son, Isaac, and Isaac's descendants:

> *Then the Lord appeared to him and said: "Do not go down to Egypt;*
> *live in the land of which I shall tell you. Dwell in this land, and I will*
> *be with you and bless you; for to you and your descendants I give all*
> *these lands, and I will perform the oath which I swore to Abraham*
> *your father. And I will make your descendants multiply as the stars of*
> *heaven; I will give to your descendants all these lands; and in your*
> *seed all the nations of the earth shall be blessed; because Abraham*
> *obeyed My voice and kept My charge, My commandments, My*
> *statutes, and My laws" (Genesis 26:2-5).*

These verses clearly show how the blessing Abraham received is being passed to future generations. In Genesis chapter 28, we read of how the blessing is now passed to the next generation—to Isaac's son, Jacob, and to Jacob's descendants:

> *Then Isaac called Jacob and blessed him [saying]... "May God*
> *Almighty bless you, and make you fruitful and multiply you, that*
> *you may be an assembly of peoples; and give you the blessing of*
> *Abraham, to you and your descendants with you, that you may*
> *inherit the land in which you are a stranger, which God gave to*
> *Abraham" (Genesis 28:1;3-4).*

Jacob had many sons, but the one we are most familiar with is Joseph, whom he loved greatly (see Gen. 37:3). When Joseph was in Egypt, Pharaoh was greatly troubled by dreams than no one could interpret. When Joseph was called to help, he told Pharaoh, "It is not in me; God will give Pharaoh an answer of peace" (see Gen. 41:16). With God's help, Joseph was able to interpret the dreams. Joseph was recognized as "a man in whom is the Spirit of God," and he was greatly rewarded and given a position of power (see Gen. 41:38).

> *Then Pharaoh said to Joseph, "Inasmuch as God has shown you*
> *all this, there is no one as discerning and wise as you. You shall be*
> *over my house, and all my people shall be ruled according to your*
> *word; only in regard to the throne will I be greater than you." And*
> *Pharaoh said to Joseph, "See, I have set you over all the land of*
> *Egypt." Then Pharaoh took his signet ring off his hand and put it*
> *on Joseph's hand; and he clothed him in garments of fine linen and*
> *put a gold chain around his neck (Genesis 41:39-42).*

Abraham, Isaac, Jacob, and now Joseph. After four generations, the blessing was still flowing. Now let's skip forward several generations and read about Moses, a descendant of Jacob (see Exod. 2:1-2). God instructed Moses, saying:

> *Go and gather the elders of Israel together, and say to them, "The Lord God of your fathers, the God of Abraham, of Isaac, and of Jacob, appeared to me, saying, 'I have surely visited you and seen what is done to you in Egypt'"* (Exodus 3:16).

Here we see God is introducing Himself as the God of Abraham, Isaac, and Jacob. We could continue to trace the generational blessing, but I believe I have made my point. God is a generational God.

A GENERATIONAL-MINDED PEOPLE

Since God is a generational God, He expects us also to be a generational-minded people. In Proverbs, we read, "A good man leaves an inheritance to his children's children, but the wealth of the sinner is stored up for the righteous" (Prov. 13:22).

God expects our legacy, posterity, and inheritance to reach at least two generations past our lives. Our legacy should extend at least two generations after we enjoy what our existence establishes, or else we have not fulfilled the perfect plan of God and maximized our existence. I believe this is part of why God refers to Himself as the God of Abraham, Isaac, and Jacob. He could have continued, but this was a prophetic picture of Proverbs 13:22.

When we understand this generational characteristic of God and His generational expectation of us, we will become more responsible in our life. We will realize that any evil we do will affect unborn generations, and it is not evil that He expects us to pass down to succeeding generations.

Chapter 14

The Importance of Inheritance

Just as we discussed the importance of utilizing both spiritual and physical investment vehicles, it is also essential that we leave both a spiritual and physical inheritance.

What inheritance does God have in mind and expect us to leave behind? There are two kinds of inheritance. Unfortunately, imbalance in the teachings of the Church has overemphasized one kind and said little or nothing about the other. God was speaking of both *spiritual and physical inheritance*, just as we have both spiritual and physical vehicles of wealth creation.

Dictionaries tend to define *inheritance* only in regards to physical inheritance. According to the *Oxford Advanced Learner's Dictionary, inherit* means "to receive money or property as a result of the owner's death." *Inheritance* means "the act of inheriting something from someone."

Vines Expository Dictionary brings a spiritual dimension to the definition of inheritance by describing it as a "birthright." A *birthright* is "a possession you enter into by virtue of birth into a family; something you receive as a gift and not a reward for keeping a law; what you receive on the condition of obedience to certain instructions." In Genesis, we read:

> *And the Lord said, "Shall I hide from Abraham what I am doing, since Abraham shall surely become a great and mighty nation, and all the nations of the earth shall be blessed in him? For I have known him, in order that he may command his children and his household after him, that they keep the way of the Lord, to do*

righteousness and justice, that the Lord may bring to Abraham what He has spoken to him" (Genesis 18:17-19).

Here we see that God expected and believed that Abraham would leave a spiritual inheritance for his children. The New International Version says, "For I have chosen him, so that he will direct his children and his household after him to keep the way of the Lord by doing what is right and just" (see Gen. 18:19 NIV).

Spiritual Inheritance

What do we mean when we say "spiritual inheritance"? What does it include? Spiritual inheritance means seeing the next generation saved and connected to God in a personal covenant relationship. It means teaching the next generation the power of prayer, the Word of God, and how to study the Word. Spiritual inheritance includes laying a solid, balanced foundation and passing on God's moral principles to the next generation. It also involves leaving a good name for those who come after you. Finally, it includes teaching them about financial intelligence and an investment mentality.

In Genesis, we read, "And Abraham gave all that he had to Isaac" (Gen. 25:5). Abraham not only gave spiritual inheritance, but also physical inheritance. All his wealth and estate went to Isaac as an inheritance. Abraham's ceiling was Isaac's foundation. But even with all that Abraham gave to Isaac, we still find Isaac farming but broke and planning to run to Egypt until God intervenes (see Gen. 26:1-5). If we give wealth to the next generation, but they cannot manage it, our labor has been in vain.

Physical Inheritance

What do we mean when we say "physical inheritance"? It includes many things, such as: real estate, stocks or paper assets, businesses, cash, or other material possessions. Just as we discussed earlier the importance of utilizing both spiritual and physical investment vehicles, it is also essential that we leave both spiritual and physical inheritances. To leave one without the other is incomplete.

I encourage you to consider what inheritance you are leaving for your children and for those who come after them. Apart from your inheritance in Christ, what other inheritance do you have both spiritually and physically?

LESSONS FROM THE STORY OF THE WIDOW

The Book of Second Kings records a very sad story of what can happen to God's children—even to His ministers—when they lack financial intelligence:

> *A certain woman of the wives of the sons of the prophets cried out to Elisha, saying, "Your servant my husband is dead, and you know that your servant feared the Lord. And the creditor is coming to take my two sons to be his slaves." So Elisha said to her, "What shall I do for you? Tell me, what do you have in the house?" And she said, "Your maidservant has nothing in the house but a jar of oil." Then he said, "Go, borrow vessels from everywhere, from all your neighbors—empty vessels; do not gather just a few. And when you have come in, you shall shut the door behind you and your sons; then pour it into all those vessels, and set aside the full ones." So she went from him and shut the door behind her and her sons, who brought the vessels to her; and she poured it out. Now it came to pass, when the vessels were full, that she said to her son, "Bring me another vessel." And he said to her, "There is not another vessel." So the oil ceased. Then she came and told the man of God. And he said, "Go, sell the oil and pay your debt; and you and your sons live on the rest"* (2 Kings 4:1-7).

In this story, we read how a widow and her sons are in debt even though her husband feared the Lord. They were in dire straights; a creditor was coming to take her sons into slavery. Fortunately for this family, God stepped in through Elisha and saved them from their distress.

Proverbs warns us not to be foolish. This includes foolishness regarding both spiritual and physical inheritance. We are told, "There is desirable treasure, and oil in the dwelling of the wise, but a foolish man squanders it" (Prov. 21:20). To live without saving or investing and to spend all we make is foolishness.

Proverbs also instructs on the importance of planning and being diligent. "The plans of the diligent lead surely to plenty, but those of everyone who is hasty, surely to poverty" (Prov. 21:5). To be diligent means to think and plan how to multiply what you have with an investment mentality.

In the story found in Second Kings, the prophet died, leaving only debt for his children. He was unable to take care of his family, and even worse, he had used his children (his future, the next generation) as collateral for a loan. That he did this indicates that he had no other assets to use as collateral.

And yet this man feared God. He operated in the office of a prophet. He had spiritual covering. This only goes to prove what I have been emphasizing in this book—*the spiritual is not complete without the physical.*

What would make a man borrow money and use his children as collateral? I pray that we may never be reduced to that level. The man definitely failed in his responsibilities, but what part did his wife play? What was she doing when her children were being pledged as collateral for a loan? After her husband died, why did she not find a way to settle the debt? Why did she wait to seek help until the creditor was coming to take her sons?

If we look more closely at this story, we can see that both the prophet and his wife were responsible, in part, for the situation. We have already discussed the man's poor choices to acquire debt and use his children as collateral. We have also mentioned that the widow failed to act earlier to repay the debt. In verse 2, we see that she said she had nothing but a jar of oil. When people focus on what they do not have, they fail to maximize the potential of what they do have. In verse 3, she was advised to create room and create opportunity (to borrow vessels) to use what she had (oil). Elisha was encouraging her to think big when he instructed her to gather more than just a few vessels.

In verse 4, the widow was advised to become an entrepreneur, to trade what she had and become a marketer of oil. This may be stretching things a bit, but consider my interpretations of these phrases:

- "Shut the door" refers to trade secrets and entrepreneurship.

- "Pour into vessels" refers to production and manufacturing.
- "Set aside the full ones" refers to product management and storage.

In verse 5, we see that the widow obeyed Elisha's instructions. In verse 6, we see that her mentality limited her productivity. Elisha instructed her to "not gather just a few," yet her mind could not handle the big things God had in store (see 2 Kings 4:3). Having too few vessels also reveals that she was relationally poor; she had limited friends within her network and so had limited vessels. Opportunities in life are limited to your networks.

In verse 7, the widow was advised to sell the oil, pay her debt, and live on the rest with her sons. Simply put, Elisha taught her financial intelligence and entrepreneurship to change her story. Again, this may be stretching things a bit, but consider the truths revealed in his words:

- "Sell" encompasses knowing how to market yourself, your gift, your services or product.
- "Pay your debt" relates to learning financial management principles.
- "Live on the rest" indicates financial planning—living within your means.

Elisha was able to solve all the problems that the man and his widow could not. He did this not by prayer and fasting, nor by giving her money. Instead he taught her an investment mentality and how to use what she had to get what she needed.

This book in your hand is ordained to do the same in your life. As I have said before, it is not what you do not have that matters, but what you do with what you have.

FULL-TIME OR FOOL-TIME

After over seventeen years in ministry and many encounters with God and His Word, I have come to realize that a majority of ministers, who claim to be in full-time ministry, are fooling themselves. I have seen how in the name of full-time ministry, many ministers have opened the door for poverty to ravage their lives, their marriages, their children, and even their so-called ministry. I have realized that this full-time foolishness has become an umbrella under which many lazy ministers hide, and many of them have subjected their families to serious suffering. Some of them have lost their marriages, their children, and more.

I do not want to delve too deeply into this issue, but if you are in full-time ministry, I encourage you to consider the following questions:

- Did God really tell you to go into full-time ministry without doing any other job, or did you hear a deceiving voice of man?

- Is the church or ministry you oversee big enough to pay you to handle your family responsibilities, without you becoming an irresponsible husband and father?

- Is the church or ministry work presently enough to occupy all your time (is it a full-time position)?

- If God told you not to do any "business" that would take your time or distract you from your calling and assignment, did He also tell you not to invest in shares, real estate, or intellectual properties, which take less time and are less distracting?

- If man did not fall and there was no need for the five-fold ministry, what would you be doing with your life?

- Are you really sure that God's perfect will for you is to live the way you are living?

- Have you asked your mentors if they have invested in shares, real estate, business, or intellectual property? Perhaps they can guide you in this regard.

I am not God, and I do not claim to know more than you, but I strongly encourage you to think these points through so that you do not end up like the prophet in Second Kings. I want to make clear that I am not against full-time ministry if the size of the ministry demands it and an investment mentality is in place.

WEALTH TRANSFER—WEALTH OF THE WICKED

I have already mentioned several imbalances that I believe are prevalent in the teachings of the Church today. Another imbalance I would like to address is regarding the teaching on wealth transfer. Wealth transfer used to be a very popular teaching some years ago, and it seems to have resurrected again. Many ministries have started teaching that the wealth of the wicked is coming to the righteous. They base this on the second half of a verse which says, "the wealth of the sinner is stored up for the righteous" (see Prov. 13:22).

In earlier waves of this teaching, people were taught what God's wealth transfer agenda was, but they were never taught how this agenda would become a reality. This made people enter into the error of laziness and covetousness. Some people went so far as to tell rich non-Christians that all they were laboring for would come to them. Some people even went to others' houses, took pictures, and started claiming them.

I believe in the Bible. I believe in the wealth transfer agenda. But I believe there is a technology God has put in place for this to happen, and unless we teach people the "how"—the technology of wealth transfer—we will only excite ourselves and stay in the same place.

Let's look again at Proverbs, but this time let's look at the whole verse. It says, "A good man leaves an inheritance to his children's children, but the wealth of the sinner is stored up for the righteous" (Prov. 13:22). Our focus should be on the first part, not the second part. As we concentrate on applying all the principles this book has revealed, and as we begin to put necessary vehicles in place to settle our generation and the succeeding ones, we will be empowered and have the opportunity to experience the wealth transfer.

The power to get wealth, the spiritual vehicles, and the physical vehicles must all come together to operate as the "how"—the technology of wealth transfer. Let me give you some examples of wealth transfer to prove that the *power to get wealth* and the *vehicles of wealth* are the technology for wealth transfer.

An Unwanted Mansion

Once a man built a huge mansion, but it became haunted. No one could live in it. He tried to get rid of the house, but no one was willing to buy it. Then he was introduced to a church, and he sought help from the pastor. The pastor got a prayer group together, and they went to the house to pray. While they were praying, a large python and several

149

smaller snakes fell from the ceiling. The group fled but later returned to keep praying, until the python and the smaller snakes were subdued and killed.

As the prayer group was leaving, the man said that he no longer needed the house because he could not imagine living in it after what he had experienced. It took prayer, opportunity, choice, the Word, the anointing, and the seeds of the past for that minister to experience a wealth transfer opportunity of a "house of the wicked." If he had not had the spiritual power to deal with the problem, he would not have had that opportunity.

A Great Business Opportunity

Once a man labored to buy properties and start a business. Due to his "Christ-less" situation, the enemy attacked and the man then wanted to sell off all his properties and business at a ridiculously low price. A covenant believer, with ready cash, was able to take over everything. It took opportunity and ready cash to experience that wealth transfer. What if the believer had not had ready cash?

Wealth Transfer Not as God Intended

Many believers do not have the vehicles of wealth transfer in place. In my opinion, if there is any wealth transfer occurring now, it is more likely to be the wealth of the righteous going to the wicked. Let me explain by asking you to consider these questions:

- Is your landlord a tithe-paying believer?

- Was your car bought from a tithe-paying believer?

- Is your fuel bought from a tithe-paying believer?

- Are your food items bought from a tithe-paying believer?

- Are your clothes bought from a tithe-paying believer?

- Are your electronics bought from a tithe-paying believer?

- Are your furniture items bought from a tithe-paying believer?

If the majority of what you buy comes from non-Christians, then every day your money is being transferred to the wicked. It is time for churches and Christians to start businesses and to buy businesses in order be in a position for wealth transfer. Remember, in order for Abraham to possess Canaan, he bought into it. There is wealth transfer, but there is a technology to make it happen.

If you apply all you have learned in this book, you will not need to worry about the wealth of the wicked because you will already have your own wealth. But by applying these principles regarding the power to get wealth and spiritual and physical investment vehicles, you will be in a position to experience wealth transfer.

If everyone lived like the prophet we read about in Second Kings, then how would God's purpose on earth be fulfilled? The prophet died without leaving anything good for his children, both spiritually and physically.

Proverbs says, "Train up a child in the way he should go, and when he is old he will not depart from it. The rich rules over the poor, and the borrower is servant to the lender" (Prov. 22:6-7). Part of training is to let our children know how to manage money and avoid debt so that debt will not put them in bondage to other people. If we cannot live debt-free, how can we teach what we do not know?

HOW FAR WITH US?

It is easy to read the stories of others and blame them, but many of us are already moving in a direction that would make us end up like them unless we change our mentality, our attitudes, and our lifestyle.

> *The word of the Lord came to me again, saying, "What do you mean when you use this proverb concerning the land of Israel, saying: 'The fathers have eaten sour grapes, and the children's teeth are set on edge'?"* (Ezekiel 18:1-2)

Do not blame your father or predecessors for everything. They have lived their lives; it is now your turn to prove yourself. Your father may not have left any inheritance for you. The question now is, what are you going to leave behind for the next generation? Do not repeat the mistakes of your father; secure the future of your children. In Psalms it says:

> *I have been young, and now am old; yet I have not seen the righteous forsaken, nor his descendants begging bread. He is ever merciful, and lends; and his descendants are blessed* (Psalm 37:25-26).

Can this Scripture be fulfilled in your generation? Was your father "the righteous"? Are you "the righteous" who will activate this Scripture? Are you the seed of the righteous who should not beg for bread? Will your seed beg for bread? May the grace of God make you a testimony of this Scripture.

WHO SHOULD INHERIT FROM WHOM?

Is it the children who should inherit from their parents or the parents who should inherit from their children? Consider what it says in Second Corinthians:

> *Now for the third time I am ready to come to you. And I will not be burdensome to you; for I do not seek yours, but you. For the children ought not to lay up for the parents, but the parents for the children* (2 Corinthians 12:14).

Some parents tend to train their children as if it is the responsibility of the children to grow up, work, and leave an inheritance for them. But God expects parents to leave an inheritance for their children, not the other way around. To saddle your children with the responsibility of feeding you, clothing you, and housing you means you are living below God's plan for your life. I believe children should bless their parents—as I explained earlier under the spiritual vehicles of wealth creation—but this does not mean children should have to sustain their parents.

Pray and work toward being a blessing and leaving an inheritance for your children so that you will not be a liability to your children. If you have the mind-set that you are training them now so that they can sustain you when they grow up, I encourage you to change that mentality and start planning your life.

TIME TO ACTIVATE GENERATIONAL BLESSINGS

In light of all we have learned about inheritance, let us now consider activating generational blessings. Unborn generations are waiting to benefit from our existence on earth today. It is time to activate generational blessings. God is a generational God. The earth He created is still in existence, the humanity He created is still in existence—all because God sustains what He creates and makes it transcend generations.

Many organizations have transcended generations and become part of posterity. Companies like Mercedes-Benz, Ford, Honda, Coca-Cola, and others have existed for decades. In religious circles, the Catholic Church, the Foursquare Church, the Church of God in Christ, the Assemblies of God, and others have existed for decades.

What are you putting in place to bless the next generation? In order to activate generational blessings:

- We must develop a kingdom mentality.

- We must develop a posterity mentality.

- We must eradicate toxic mentalities.

- We must develop an investment mentality.

- We must establish investment vehicles.

- We must create and perpetuate wealth.

I believe everything I have shared so far can equip us to do so. It time to act!

Chapter 15

Final Thoughts

*The price you fail to pay today will be
paid tomorrow with interest.*

Having come this far, I would like to use this chapter to share some final thoughts with you.

WINDOWS OF OPPORTUNITY

First, I want to describe three examples of wealth creation vehicles operating in Nigeria. I encourage you to seek out opportunities like these where you can practice the principles you have learned and see results.

The Fingerprint Investment Club

The Fingerprint Investment Club is an initiative of Common Sense Ltd., a company I presently have the privilege to head as the CEO. After many years of teaching investment principles, I—along with other experienced and highly versatile investors—have discovered that many people need those they can trust to help set up and administer investment vehicles.

The Fingerprint Investment Club is our way of helping people become wealthy. It is an investment club aimed at motivating, guiding, and assisting others to invest their money wisely. The club utilizes the principles of developing financial intelligence, planning, and discipline to help others reach their goals.

Common Sense Estate Development

Another window of opportunity is Common Sense Estate Development. The primary purpose of this project is to make affordable land available to interested individuals, both for residential and commercial purposes. We buy large expanses of land, sell individual plots to others, and together we develop a fully functional residential estate. This company oversees buying land and selling plots and building and managing developments in order to help others build wealth through real estate. The project has overseen two such estates so far—one of 50 acres and another of 70 acres. By the time you are reading this, the number may have increased.

Common Sense Training, Seminars, and Consultancy

This company offers training, seminars, and consulting covering the scope of this book and more. Such programs have been provided to churches, organizations, corporations, civil servants, students, and others. We currently have over twenty books and products available. We provide opportunities for others to market and distribute these products as a way for them to build wealth.

These and other such windows of opportunity are available. You simply need to look for them. If you would like more information about the specific vehicles mentioned, please contact me.

A TOOL TO GUIDE YOU

I have no doubt in my heart that this book has affected you positively, since I have been affected positively by the truths shared in this book. Writing this book has been a refreshing time for me. And the book is not over yet.

I have included a bonus workbook for you. It contains questions to help keep the principles in your heart and mind. It also contains guidelines for practicing the truths and principles shared, to help make them a part of your life. Please do not ignore the workbook; it is very powerful. But before you turn to it, I would like you to consider a few final thoughts.

How Will Your Death Be Announced?

Something that is common to all is that we are all born, and we will all die one day. When you die, how will your death be announced? I believe that what you do with the information you have learned from this book will determine how your death will be announced. Consider this announcement:

> *It is with deep sorrow of heart, we regret to announce the passing of* [your name], *whose demise occurred on* [date]. [Your name] *is survived by* [names of family members].

This kind of announcement shows a death that leaves pain and sorrow for those left behind. Crying, wailing, and anguish characterize this kind of burial because the dead, most likely, left nothing substantial behind. Now consider a different kind of announcement:

> *With gratitude to God for a life well spent, we announce the passing away into glory of our* [your name]. *May* [your name]*'s gentle soul rest in perfect peace.* [Your name] *is survived by* [names of family members].

This kind of announcement shows a death that leaves something behind. At this kind of burial people do not cry, wail, or show anguish because there is no inheritance. They cry because the dead is missed, but they recognize that he or she had a life well spent, with great inheritance left behind for others to enjoy.

Do you want to die and leave your family and offspring in pain, or do you want to exit with eternal legacies in place? The Book of Mark asks, "For what will it profit a man if he gains the whole world, and loses his own soul?" (Mark 8:36).

God wants us to have all the best the world has to offer and live in stupendous wealth, but it is all based on the premise that the spiritual has been put in place. To gain the whole world and lose our soul is to lose everything. We came into this world with nothing, and we are definitely going back with nothing.

When we die, our life's journey will be characterized by a dash. What do I mean by this? Think of what a death announcement or a tombstone looks like. They usually include the name of the deceased and the date of his birth and death, separated by a dash. All the person's qualifications, achievements, investments, and so on are only represented by that dash. The life we live now will determine what our dash will be interpreted to mean.

FINDING PEACE WITH GOD

A life without Christ is meaningless. In order to find peace with God, you need to embrace God's love and receive the salvation that only Jesus Christ gives. There are some basic steps to take to usher in a world of new beginnings.

Recognize your need for God. As it says in Romans, "For all have sinned and fall short of the glory of God" (Rom. 3:23). We all have need of a Savior, and in order to succeed in life, we need God.

Repent of your sins. In First John we read, "If we confess our sins, He is faithful and just to forgive us our sins and to cleanse us from all unrighteousness" (1 John 1:9). Sin creates a wall between man and God, which hinders God from being able to intervene on our behalf in different areas of life. However, repentance opens a door to God.

Believe in Jesus. The Book of John tells us, "For God so loved the world that He gave His only begotten Son, that whoever believes in Him should not perish but have everlasting life" (John 3:16). Jesus is God's only way to salvation, and believing in what Jesus did on Calvary gives us access to salvation.

Receive His salvation. Again in John we read, "But as many as received Him, to them He gave the right to become children of God, to those who believe in His name" (John 1:12). It is one thing for someone to offer you a gift; it is another thing for you to receive it. God has offered us the gift of salvation through His Son Jesus, but we must receive and accept Him.

Confess your faith. The Book of Romans tells us:

> *...if you confess with your mouth the Lord Jesus and believe in your heart that God has raised Him from the dead, you will be saved. For with the heart one believes unto righteousness, and with the mouth confession is made unto salvation* (Romans 10:9-10).

If you have not done so already, I encourage you to make a confession of what you believe and begin to walk in newness of life. Pray the following prayer with faith and believe God to do His work in you as you pray:

> *Heavenly Father, I thank you for the gift of Your Son Jesus! Lord, I believe in my heart that You died on the cross to redeem me and You rose again to justify me. Come into my life, Lord Jesus and make me whole. Cleanse me by Your blood, and deliver me by Your power. In my life, let the power of the wicked fail and let Your Spirit take over. Thank You for saving me. Amen.*

If you have prayed this prayer sincerely from your heart, welcome to a new level of life! I would like to hear from you. I encourage you to write and share your story with me. If you would like, I can send you free literature and materials that will help you grow in God.

I would also like to stand in agreement with you concerning any areas of your life where you need God's intervention. Feel free to share with me about areas where you need prayer, and I will be glad to pray along with you.

Finally, if this book has affected you positively in any way, please feel free to get in touch with me. I would like to hear any questions or comments you have. You are special to me, and hearing from you will be a thing of joy. Shalom!

WORKBOOK

I will stand my watch and set myself on the rampart, and watch to see what He will say to me, and what I will answer when I am corrected (Habakkuk 2:1).

INTRODUCTION

Many people have read numerous books but have lacked the ability to get the best out of these books. This can occur for many reasons, such as:

- inability to understand a book;

- failure to apply the information from a book;

- inability to internalize the principles in a book and plan their use.

This workbook is designed to help you internalize the principles revealed in this book. It should also help you to review the material to gain deeper insight and understanding. Using this workbook should encourage you to take action and apply what you have learned. I strongly encourage you to use this workbook as a tool to guide you to greater wealth.

Please begin by completing the Financial Intelligence Questionnaire (FIQ) again. This time, fill it out in light of what you have learned in this book. I recommend that you complete the FIQ at least once every year as a way to check your financial pulse and progress.

POVERTY REDEFINED

State the four definitions of poverty.

_____

_____

_____

_____

_____

State the seven dimensions of poverty.

_____

_____

_____

_____

_____

Describe your view about the definitions and dimensions of poverty. This will help you to internalize these truths.

_____

_____

_____

_____

_____

_____

_____

UNIVERSAL CAUSES OF POVERTY

List the seven universal causes of poverty.

_____

_____

_____

_____

_____

Which of them really affects and relates to you?

_____

_____

_____

_____

_____

Describe practical steps you intend to take to change your current state.

_____

_____

_____

_____

_____

_____

FIVE TOXIC MENTALITIES

List the five toxic mentalities.

_____

_____

_____

_____

_____

Which of them directly applies to you?

_____

_____

_____

_____

What practical steps have you established to change your mentality where needed?

_____

_____

_____

_____

_____

_____

DEVELOPING AN INVESTMENT MENTALITY

What is an investment mentality?

_____

_____

_____

_____

_____

What three things can you do with money?

_____

_____

_____

_____

_____

Under which category do you belong and why?

_____

_____

_____

_____

_____

_____

MENTALITY SHAPERS

What are the seven things that can shape mentality?

_____

_____

_____

_____

_____

_____

_____

_____

_____

How do any or all of these affect you, and what are you doing about it?

_____

_____

_____

_____

_____

_____

_____

_____

_____

_____

The Power to Get Wealth

What was your understanding of "the power to get wealth" before reading this book, and what is your understanding now?

_____

_____

_____

_____

_____

Describe the seven powers to get wealth.

_____

_____

_____

_____

What steps do you intend to take to use this power for wealth creation in your life?

_____

_____

_____

_____

_____

_____

_____

THE PATHWAY TO WEALTH—
FINANCIAL INTELLIGENCE

State the three steps of the pathway to wealth.

_____

_____

_____

_____

_____

Define these three steps in your own words.

_____

_____

_____

_____

This book presented a view of formal education. In what way has this book helped you differently from your school or formal education?

_____

_____

_____

_____

_____

_____

_____

The Pathway to Wealth—
Financial Planning

Describe the three stages of life.

_____

_____

_____

_____

_____

Have you been able to maximize these stages, or how do you intend to do so?

_____

_____

_____

_____

_____

Have you ascertained your present location on the pathway to wealth? In answering this question, please address the following issues:

Present Age: _____

Total Debt: _____

Total Assets: _____

Present Income Sources: _____

Possible Income Sources: _____

Have you determined your destination? In answering this question, please address the following issues:

Retirement Age:_____

Financial Level at Retirement:_____

Quality of Life Expected:_____

_____

Retirement Plan:_____

_____

State the vehicles you intend to use:

_____

_____

_____

Do you fully understand the 30:70 principle? If not, go back review it. Then describe it here in your own words.

_____

_____

_____

What steps are you planning to take to implement the 30:70 principle?

_____

_____

_____

_____

_____

Do you have a budget in place? Does it account for monthly, quarterly, and annual expenses and income?

_____

_____

_____

_____

_____

_____

_____

What types of income do you presently have in place?

Earned:_____

Portfolio:_____

Passive:_____

Describe your understanding of the following and how they affect investments:

Planning:_____

_____

Time:_____

_____

Inflation:_____

_____

Compound Interest:_____

_____

The Power of Annuity:_____

_____

THE PATHWAY TO WEALTH— FINANCIAL DISCIPLINE

Do you consider yourself to be a disciplined person financially? If not, how do you intend to effect a change?

What is Parkinson's Law, and how do you plan to rise above it in your life?

What steps do you intend to take to reduce your expenditures and liabilities?

SPIRITUAL VEHICLES OF WEALTH CREATION

Describe ten spiritual vehicles of wealth creation.

_____

_____

_____

_____

_____

_____

_____

_____

Have you been faithful to invest in these spiritual vehicles? If not, why?

_____

_____

_____

_____

_____

_____

_____

_____

_____

_____

PHYSICAL VEHICLES
OF WEALTH CREATION

Describe ten physical vehicles of wealth creation.

_____

_____

_____

_____

This book discussed the difference between being an employee or an employer. Which are you, and what are your plans for the future?

_____

_____

_____

_____

_____

_____

Which of the physical vehicles do you already have in place, and which of them do you intend to put in place for your journey to wealth?

_____

_____

_____

_____

_____

MULTIPLE STREAMS OF INCOME

Describe the categories of income streams.

_____

_____

_____

_____

What income streams do you currently have in place?

_____

_____

_____

_____

What strategies and steps do you have in place to create multiple streams of income in your life?

_____

_____

_____

_____

_____

_____

_____

_____

ACTIVATING GENERATIONAL BLESSINGS

What is your understanding of generational blessings and curses?

_____

_____

_____

_____

What makes God a generational God?

_____

_____

_____

_____

_____

Why are we called to be a generational-minded people? What does God expect?

_____

_____

_____

_____

_____

THE IMPORTANCE OF INHERITANCE

Describe the inheritance you have from your parents or grandparents, both physical and spiritual.

_____

_____

_____

_____

What is your understanding of wealth transfer?

_____

_____

_____

_____

_____

What steps have you put in place to leave an inheritance for your children and grandchildren?

_____

_____

_____

_____

_____

FINAL THOUGHTS

Have you begun to seek out windows of opportunity where you can apply the principles you have learned in this book? If so, describe what you have found. If not, what's stopping you?

_____

_____

_____

_____

_____

_____

How do you think your death will be announced?

_____

_____

_____

_____

_____

_____

If you do not have a relationship with God, I encourage you to reread the final section of the last chapter about finding peace with God. I wish you peace and prosperity. Shalom!

Other Books by the Author

- Singles Thou Art Loosed
- Breaking the Strongholds of Delay
- Love Is Not Enough
- Common Sense Is Not Common
- Are You a Fool? A Question or an Insult?
- Why Are You Not Married?
- 101 Wisdom for Singles
- 101 Answers for Singles
- Singles Get Ready
- Friends and Friendship
- The Power of Mercy

Mini Book Series by the Author

- Maximizing Opportunities
- Developing a Reading Culture
- Building Strong Self-Esteem
- Overcoming the Excuses of Failure
- Overcoming the Forces of Limitation
- The Making of a Dream
- Singles, No More Games!
- Living Above Average
- When No One Believes You

CONTACT THE AUTHOR

If you wish to contact the Author, please write to:

Olumide Emmanuel
PO Box 2847
Ikeja, Lagos
NIGERIA

commonsense2006@yahoo.com
olumideoo@yahoo.com

THE BUSINESS OFFICE
FOR COMMON SENSE LTD.

5 Osho Street
(off Opebi Road, along the Oregun
Link Bridge Road)
Ikeja, Lagos
NIGERIA

Or call these numbers:

LAGOS, NIGERIA	UNITED KINGDOM	UNITED STATES
+234 1 4710498	+44 7790789724	+1 770 3808414
+234 1 4362747	+44 07904273503	
+234 8033208813		

Or reach us on the Internet:
www.commonsenseonline.org
www.cbcnigeria.org

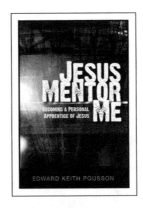

Additional copies of this book and other book titles from DESTINY IMAGE™ EUROPE are available at your local bookstore.

We are adding new titles every month!

To view our complete catalog online, visit us at:
www.eurodestinyimage.com

Send a request for a catalog to:

Via Acquacorrente, 6
65123 - Pescara - ITALY
Tel. +39 085 4716623 - Fax +39 085 9431270

"Changing the world, one book at a time."

Are you an author?

Do you have a today, God-given message?

CONTACT US

We will be happy to review your manuscript for the possibility of publication:

publisher@eurodestinyimage.com
http://www.eurodestinyimage.com/pages/AuthorsAppForm.htm